ADVANCE PRAISE

"The tools and practices in *Be a Better Team by Friday* are exactly what any M&A venture needs to deal with the conflicts that arise when bringing together two or more company cultures. BLUECASE proved essential in supporting our integration of two companies by giving us the tools to create a unified culture and leadership approach. Before BLUECASE, our acquisition wasn't going well, and the two companies became siloed, which caused communication and trust challenges. With Justin and David's guidance, we quickly strengthened our culture, moved faster, and achieved our goals. BLUECASE deserves its stellar reputation, and I enthusiastically recommend them, especially to companies looking to integrate cultures post-M&A."

—MATT MURPHY, Co-founder and Partner
of Astra Capital Management

"We've been on one hell of a ride with BLUECASE! David and Justin have become trusted advisors who've supported us through thirteen acquisitions, growing our customer base from 500 to over 10,000, expanding our team from 50 to over 400, and growing from one location to five. The foundational work we've done with David and Justin grew our capabilities to take our workforce fully remote during the pandemic. BLUECASE has been one of our top resources during COVID-19, hands down. We've integrated many of the tools and practices in this book into day-to-day operations across our company. As a result, our culture and leadership have grown stronger as we have scaled."

—CHRIS DILLIE, CEO of ESO Solutions

"*Be a Better Team by Friday* is an accurate title—the tools in this book really do lead to immediate results that make a big difference. As the CEO forming one of the largest public infrastructure services companies in the US, I relied on Justin and David to help me align merging teams under one umbrella. Usually, building this level of trust can take years, but BLUECASE laid the foundation in a couple of days. My team still reflects on how important that foundational work has been to our current leadership culture. Justin and David encouraged me to be an authentic, heart-led CEO to identify and model our core values and speak my vision. Over the years, our coaching relationship has turned into genuine camaraderie, deep respect, and friendship."

—**L. JOE BOYER**, CEO of ATLAS

"BLUECASE makes work more fun! David and Justin gave us the practical tools to significantly improve our communication to move faster, make better decisions, and align more closely with our goals. Marketing, sales, and development teams all speak the same language now, and we're no longer talking past each other when collaborating. This shared language makes integrating new managers and executive team members nearly seamless. BLUECASE's expertise has been invaluable to our company's success. I'd recommend this book to any CEO who cares deeply about growing quickly *and* strengthening the culture they worked so hard to create."

—**AMY PORTER**, Founder and Executive Chairman of AffiniPay

"Read this book if you want to see your organization change in real time! Before BLUECASE, we had two cultures—an engineering culture and a business culture. I tried everything I knew to create cohesion but was near my breaking point. Employees perceived me as disengaged, and morale was at an all-time low. When a friend introduced me to Justin and David, I was skeptical about whether they could help us bridge the cultural divide. Other programs had offered short-term improvements, but nothing ever stuck. BLUECASE surprised me—they delivered on everything they said they'd do. After our first session with Justin and David, we were a better team, just like the book promises. Their approach profoundly energized and bonded the team, resulting in a seismic cultural shift I never thought possible. Over two years, they helped us address company-wide breakdowns, grow, and, eventually, sell the company to one of the largest fintech companies in the world."

—BRANDON LLOYD, Former CEO of Bypass

"We'd positioned ourselves for growth and taken on all the costs necessary to invest in scaling our company, and then we stayed flat for two years. We had smart, capable people on the team, but we lacked clear alignment around a comprehensive strategy and plan for execution. BLUECASE is serious about transformation. BLUECASE took risks with us to reframe our perspectives and enact real change. The results were clear—we tripled the size of our company while significantly improving the culture and collaboration. Justin and David are savvy guides, great coaches, and trusted advisors. Listen to what they have to say!"

—JR CARTER, Founder of Intersys Consulting

"As a serial entrepreneur, I have worked with many management consultants and coaches, but I recommend BLUECASE to any CEO who wants immediate, actionable insight to scale fast. BLUECASE strengthened the trust in our team so we could have the difficult conversations and productive friction that results in bold moves and extraordinary results. The BLUECASE leadership approach Justin and David lay out in this book was instrumental in elevating my entire executive team's performance. It has been several years since I retired as CEO, and I still reach out, ask for their counsel, and readily refer them."

—KATIE MAY, board member of Stamps.com and Thinkific Labs, former CEO of Shippingeasy.com, and Founder and CEO of Kidspot.com.au

"BLUECASE has earned the trust of every single one of our executive team members. David and Justin spent a lot of time and effort getting to know us individually and as a company, and now we view BLUECASE as part of our executive team. The BLUECASE practices shared in this book have helped us create a shared language and set of practices that have catapulted us to new heights we could not envision before. The financial results have been phenomenal, and we consistently outperform our peers on all of our cultural and engagement metrics. Hiring BLUECASE has been one of the best decisions I have made at SKYGEN. The leadership, coaching, and strategic planning work makes a big impact today and sets us up to realize our long-term vision. We see BLUECASE as a trusted partner and an integral part of our success."

—CRAIG KASTEN, Managing Member of SKYGEN USA

"I consider BLUECASE among the best leadership and strategy consultants I've seen in my entire career. Working with them drastically improved my performance as a CEO, and I genuinely hope we can continue our collaboration at my new company. The tools you'll find in this book have helped my team move faster, innovate more, and outperform our competitors. Beyond these tools, BLUECASE taught us how to be a high-functioning team and to dream of goals beyond what we could see at the moment. BLUECASE was an absolute game-changer for my team and me."

—JEFF SCHMALBACH, Chief Consulting Officer
of Apex Systems

"Running a business and dealing with everyday operational concerns can lead us to lose sight of the fundamentals. BLUECASE gave us a framework and structure to drive closer alignment with our strategic plan. Justin and David are excellent teachers and provided the fresh set of eyes we needed to get clear on our next steps. We grew tremendously in just nine short months. Five years later, even after selling the company, I still practice the BLUECASE tools suggested in this book because they're both sophisticated and practical. They've made me a better CEO, husband, and father. I recommend BLUECASE without hesitation."

—JUSTIN MORTARA, former CEO of Mortara Instrument

"Thanks to BLUECASE, Tailos is in the best position ever to accomplish our ambitious vision. We experienced explosive growth shortly after our Series A funding led by Octave Ventures, causing significant collaboration issues within our team. Justin and David helped me aggressively scale operations, secure funding from RB, the parent company of Lysol, and build a culture I wanted to be a part of myself. I'm excited again to go to work every day! BLUECASE's tools have been nothing short of transformative in setting us up for success. I only wish we started working with BLUECASE sooner. Don't make the same mistake—read this book!"

—MICAH GREEN, Founder and CEO of Tailos

"Our company grew remarkably in its early days before hitting a wall and stalling out. We repeatedly tried to ignite forward momentum but felt we were going in circles. When I was referred to BLUECASE, I was cynical about hiring consultants and doubted whether they could make a difference. However, in short order BLUECASE demonstrated that their approach was profoundly different. They were players on our team with remarkable listening skills and a killer tool chest. After the first meeting with my skeptical executive team, there was a new energy and attitude as the skeptics became believers. And this launched a whole new level of performance at the company. We now have this new runway to accomplish goals I never thought possible. I recommend BLUECASE and this book to any leaders who have ambitious dreams and need help closing the gap."

—TOM RHODES, Founder and CEO of Sente Mortgage

"These guys are leadership wizards! BLUECASE has given us the secret leadership code to unlock our full potential and help us scale exponentially with speed, power, and heart. The leadership tools and CEO coaching have been instrumental in getting our team in flow and securing funding from a top-tier VC firm. I feel so grateful for the opportunity to work with Justin and David and highly recommend you read this book. Trust me—they know what they're talking about."

—CT SCHENK, Co-founder and CEO of OPUS

BE A
BETTER
TEAM BY
FRIDAY

A PLAYBOOK FOR
HIGH-PERFORMANCE
BUSINESS LEADERS

JUSTIN FOLLIN
WITH DAVID BUTLEIN GREENSPAN, PHD

LIONCREST
PUBLISHING

BE A BETTER TEAM BY FRIDAY
A Playbook for High-Performance Business Leaders

First Edition: April 2023

Cover design by Sarah Brody, Chris Rorrer
Creative Direction by Caitlin McIntosh
Photography by Bailey Toksöz

ISBN   978-1-5445-3883-9   *Hardcover*
       978-1-5445-3884-6   *Paperback*
       978-1-5445-3885-3   *Ebook*

In memory of Eric Butlein, fondly known as E.B.
Father, mentor, friend, and great man.

CONTENTS

FOREWORD

by MATT BRIGGS, CEO, Four Hands

When I approached BLUECASE in 2014, I knew I needed outside help. From 2011 to 2014, my company, Four Hands, saw increases in revenue from $54M to $97M and EBITDA from $2.4M to $8.2M. Explosive growth caused many of the usual scaling challenges with company culture, performance, communication, and collaboration between teams. We tried to fix these tricky pain points of a rapidly expanding company on our own, with little success and a lot of frustration. I needed a framework to integrate new leadership under the Four Hands umbrella. I needed support with aspects of scaling my business and implementing everyday tools that would eventually lead to realizing my vision of what Four Hands could become.

I was drawn to BLUECASE founders David and Justin because their expertise in high-performance psychology and cross-functional strategic leadership offers a holistic coaching approach. I've worked with several coaches and consultants over the last twenty years who have made varying degrees of lasting contributions, but the need felt different this time. I knew we needed customized support that would penetrate throughout the organization and not just the handful of top execs. Like me, you may have had experiences with one-size-fits-all consulting approaches that are way too generic for your culture. Like me, you may have cringed at implementing processes that felt hokey or formulaic. Naturally, I had reservations.

When I first met Justin, it was immediately apparent that he possessed an extraordinary skill set paired with spot-on intuition—a rare and potent combination. Some of the most enlightening sessions with him coincided with my personal and professional lives colliding. The challenges were out of the normal scope of a business coach, and I remember wanting to cancel on Justin at least three times when I felt I didn't have the energy or space to talk with him. However, I didn't, and those were some of the most impactful coaching sessions we ever had.

Justin understands the nature and complexity of running a business like few others. He sees through superficial layers and identifies the core problem. Justin helped me consider the different ways I can add value to my company and then allocate my resources where I have the most impact. He doesn't give prescriptive advice but instead invites me to reflect more thoughtfully and make decisions from a place of clarity. He provides accountability without micromanagement. His approach is always encouraging, flexible, and solution-oriented.

Bottom line—Justin is uncommonly good at a very tough job.

The system that Justin, David, and the BLUECASE coaches brought into my company seamlessly integrates personal growth and professional leadership development. Whether I'm in a quarterly strategy session or learning a new breathing technique in one-on-one coaching, BLUECASE taught me that growth in one aspect of my life impacts all others. Whatever challenge I'm facing, BLUECASE provides deep insight, fosters creative introspection, and suggests practical solutions.

For this reason, we invest heavily in our coaching program with BLUECASE. We're putting real money behind getting the most talented coaches to work with our employees. BLUECASE is one of the best things we've done for our company, and the results speak for themselves. We've gone from $94M to half a billion in revenue since we started working with BLUECASE eight years ago. In the process, BLUECASE made our leadership team more effective. I'm excited to come to work in the morning, which benefits everyone in the company. Even better, they helped us implement a self-propagating leadership development program that consistently produces a new crop of ambitious, competent, high-performing leaders at every level.

Now, when I compare our company to others in the industry, the difference in depth of talent is staggering. The BLUECASE approach encourages team members to take ownership of arising challenges and solve them creatively. Teams fix problems autonomously, rather than taking them up the chain and requesting solutions from top management. I see true company heroes on every team.

Our level of leadership and collaboration was immeasurably enhanced with BLUECASE's guidance on internal communication issues that created unnecessary friction and frustration. BLUECASE helped us create a shared language and common terminology. We solve everyday problems more efficiently because we identify and describe them the same way instead of talking past each other and not getting anything done.

I believe the rich company culture we built with the help of BLUE-CASE is what carried us through the pandemic. We couldn't physically be together, so we needed to trust the culture we had spent so much effort building in the years before. Throughout a company's life cycle, there will be times when withdrawals from that cultural bank account far outweigh deposits. BLUECASE helped us accrue human and cultural capital reserves to thrive during a time that destroyed many other companies. Now, we can again make deposits into our cultural bank account. The next big challenge will inevitably come, but we'll be ready.

More than paid consultants, BLUECASE coaches have become invaluable, trusted guides. Making meaningful progress is challenging when you don't have a good rapport with your coach. Over the years, I've come to appreciate Justin as curious, creative, and insightful. Our mutual respect and admiration are key to making real progress. I continue to be impressed with his deep understanding of how CEOs can accelerate performance and scale their businesses while dealing with personal barriers and performance blocks.

The BLUECASE coaches working with my leadership teams mirror my experience with Justin. They are extraordinary people who add significant value to my team. I recommend BLUECASE to fellow CEOs because their approach has proved indispensable for my company's success—our financial bottom line, company culture, sustainable growth, and leadership development.

This book is a shortcut for accessing BLUECASE's leadership development process and getting to know the founders, David and Justin. If internal communications and leadership development are a source of frustration, and you struggle with company culture, enhancing creativity and innovation, or attracting the best talent—read on. You will find practical, customizable, easy-to-implement tools you can start using today.

More than advice, BLUECASE will give you the clarity you need to transform your company.

YOUR TEAM'S UNTAPPED POTENTIAL

The title of this book, *Be a Better Team by Friday*, is both an *assertion* and a *promise*.

The *assertion* is this: in a matter of a few business days, your team's performance can skyrocket. Longstanding tensions, interpersonal breakdowns, communication challenges, overwork, lack of focus, complaining, and stress can dissolve, replaced with the excitement of new possibilities. Your team can quickly propel toward goals that, until now, seemed out of reach. In just one week, you can experience a transformation from "okay" to extraordinary.

The *promise* is that the practices outlined in this book will get you there.

Of course, the gains you experience in one week are just the beginning. As we all know, a few days of exercise will make you feel good, but it takes long-term, consistent effort to get into top shape.

Just like with your personal health, creating a high-performance team requires discipline. If your team has gotten a little "soft around the middle," you're probably experiencing communication breakdowns, leadership challenges, and overall team frustrations. And you're trying to figure out what to do about it.

This book is the answer. Like a personal trainer's fitness plan for your work teams, the practices in this book make up the playbook your team needs to get back into shape.

But we want to help you do more than tighten up that soft middle. We're here to help your team reach peak performance.

Most companies that come to us feel things with their team are *pretty good*. But, in a way, that's their struggle. They're stuck in *pretty good* and don't know how to help their team reach its *full* potential. Teams in today's fast-growth companies need to adapt quickly to cross-functional projects, new hires, market fluctuations, and social changes (e.g., COVID-19) that require collaboration, accountability, ownership, and the know-how to get things done. The companies that can do this flourish. Those that don't get left behind.

Many company leaders might even see what's in their way, but don't know how to overcome the obstacles. They can't find an effective way to scale leadership beyond a select few superstars who seem more naturally skilled at leading than others. Or they have siloed teams that don't work well together—whether across acquired companies or internal departments. They want to optimize communication so that it feels like one team all running in the same direction, but they can't figure out how.

We've seen these same struggles across industries from tech and finance to healthcare and logistics. Leaders want to help their teams work together better. These leaders are smart, successful people whose entire careers are built on high performance. They're stuck, though, on how to help their teams be their best.

BLUECASE was born out of a curiosity to solve this dilemma.

As a kid, David was fascinated by superheroes. That interest continued into adulthood and evolved into a quest to understand why certain individuals and teams can do things that most of us can't. He traveled the world looking for insight. He interviewed or trained with coaches, professors, accomplished martial artists, and esteemed monks who could perform almost superhuman feats. In the process, he earned a PhD in high-performance psychology.

Having come from a family of entrepreneurs, David became frustrated by the gaps he saw in business leadership. He witnessed toxic company cultures and disheartened employees. People in power at some of the world's biggest companies weren't guiding their teams in ways that helped them be and do their best.

That frustration inspired David to ask, "What could you achieve if you combined great business practices with high-performance leadership? What if you could fill a company with leaders operating at the highest performance levels possible? Not just the CEO, but *everyone*?"

This led him into the field of management consulting, where he worked with leaders in Fortune 100 and Financial Times Stock Index (FTSI) 100 organizations, including NASA, Starbucks, Novartis, and Chevron. After accruing substantial experience working with leadership teams globally, he started BLUECASE in 2013 to formally merge high-performance psychology with strategic consulting.

He believed that if he could help businesses blend practices used by high-performing teams with leadership development and strategic planning, it could have a huge impact on the world. Organizations would be healthier. Employees would thrive at work and carry that great energy home to their families. They could achieve exceptional results *and* make people's lives better.

David couldn't create an approach to effectively scale leadership across entire companies all on his own. For this reason, he brought me in to help turn BLUECASE into a firm with the ability to scale high-level expertise and a powerful leadership methodology beyond just a few individuals at the C-suite.

By the time I partnered with David, I'd spent my career exploring questions similar to David's. I was first inspired by a pep talk I'd heard years earlier by longtime University of North Carolina Tar Heels basketball coach Roy Williams.

While still in school, I was working as a server at the UNC-Chapel Hill alumni center on the night Roy Williams and his team were there for a dinner to kick off their first game of the season. I was standing in the back of the room as Williams addressed the team. While the coach spoke, the players were hanging on his every word as if he were addressing each of them individually. I was so inspired and fired up by Williams' talk that I felt like *I* could have won a national championship.

Keep in mind, this was 2003, and Williams had taken over a Tar Heels team that had been the losingest in school history since 1962. He took that *same group of players* and turned them into NCAA champions within his second season of coaching them. It was clear that Williams had something that most people don't.

Ever since then, I've wanted to figure out: *What was that? Why do some people seem to have a unique ability to elevate groups and lead them to achieve greatness?*

I devoted the next decade to finding out. I earned a degree with a focus in business ethics (which people love to joke is an oxymoron) and studied educational and performance psychology as a teacher. I then moved to business coaching and consulting, working at a firm that was the world's largest coaching company at the time. Over the past thirteen years, I've led hundreds of executives, directors, and managers through cross-functional leadership trainings, and coached public and private CEOs, business leaders, TEDX presenters, poker players, musicians, academic professors, and athletes to perform at optimal levels. I've also designed or executed leadership development and consulting approaches delivered inside some of the world's largest oil and gas, construction, and mining companies.

David and I both discovered, in our work across industries and company sizes, that even the most well-intentioned leaders need an operating system to help their people unlock their full potential. Creating great teams is so challenging because the problems holding them back are often hard to identify or seem hard to fix. Maybe your team has interpersonal tensions, or you experience a lot of overwork but things still seem to take forever to get done. Or you suffer from "everyone's too nice," so you can't talk about what's in the way. Hidden agendas, competing priorities, lack of ownership, personality differences—even the world's best MBA programs don't prepare leaders for elusive problems like these. Your problems become more complex and complicated when growing your company at high speed. Sometimes, these challenges can seem impossible to solve.

We promise you it's not impossible. It's just that hiring great talent isn't enough. High-performing teams get that way because they *learn how to work together.* They communicate with a shared language that is easy to teach and understand. They commit to a shared set of practices that, when applied consistently, allows them to always come out on top.

You're holding those practices in your hands.

WHAT SETS HIGH-PERFORMING TEAMS APART

"Success is the product of daily habits—
not once-in-a-lifetime transformations."
—JAMES CLEAR, *Atomic Habits*

Be a Better Team by Friday contains the foundational skills and tools that turn groups of high-talent individuals into extraordinary work teams. In this book, we've consolidated these skills into seven distinct practices—field-tested techniques that will have your executive and management teams, and, ultimately, your whole organization achieve high performance.

These practices stem from our years of working with hundreds of leaders and studying the habits that help high-performance teams reach exceptional levels. As we honed our method, we were especially interested in the 80/20 approach. We wanted to know, out of all the tools that high-performing teams were using, which ones would have an emergent effect and make the biggest impact. And we've narrowed it down to these seven key practices:

1. **Choose Your Mindset**: Understand that your mindset is a choice, and that high performers choose their mindset constantly.

2. **Get Real with Each Other**: The best teams build trust by listening deeply and being direct, empathetic, and vulnerable with each other.

3. **Know the "Fundamental Why"**: High-performing teams know the underlying intent or purpose behind everything they do—and everything their team members do.

4. **Give Feedback Like a Coach**: Top performers seek out performance-enhancing feedback and share it with others every day.

5. **Adapt Your Work Style**: Agile team members adapt their communication to others, and don't expect others to conform to them. These team members learn to turn their differences into an advantage.

6. **Get Focused**: Extraordinary teams know how to pare down their workload to achieve more by doing less.

7. **Get It Done**: Very little gets done well across organizations without a plan of clear ownership and accountability. The best teams have one for everything they do.

Why do we call them practices? Because that's what great teams do: they practice getting better. Championship sports teams practice their fundamentals every day. The practices in this book are for your work teams what layups are for a basketball team: practice them regularly, and your team will improve.

And no sugar coating here—you've got to stick with them! Over time, these practices will enable your teams to achieve high levels of performance across your organization. In the companies we work with, everything from employee engagement to financial performance gets better, and the company thrives.

For this reason, we encourage you to *apply* what you read as soon as possible. We've made it straightforward and easy for you to do. Many business leaders who commit to these practices tell us the rewards extend far beyond great teams and improved organizational performance—the benefits become personal. These seven practices change lives by creating healthier, more authentic relationships with everybody you care about: your colleagues, your friends, your spouse, your family, and perhaps most importantly, yourself.

WHY YOUR COMPANY IS DRIFTING TOWARD MEDIOCRITY

Time and again, we have seen the seven practices in this book skyrocket team performance in all business environments. Over the years, we've worked with teams in almost every kind of company to help unlock their true potential. Our primary focus, however, has been partnering with fast-scaling, entrepreneurial mid-market companies, typically with annual revenues between fifty million and several billion dollars.

When we onboard a new client, we typically find that individuals across the company are working hard, but team dynamics get in the way of results. Interestingly, these dynamics tend to be universal across most companies we work with. Trust is low. People are nice to each other but avoid giving each other truthful, authentic feedback, or they criticize each other in a way that leads to defensiveness. As a group, teams generate good ideas but fail to execute. Projects get stalled (or disappear altogether).

Whether the issues stem from personality conflicts, poor communication, a lack of direction, or too much to do, team members with the best intentions simply don't know *how* to work together. The wheels spin faster and faster, and everyone works harder and harder, but as you can imagine, morale tanks when outcomes are marginal at best.

And that's just on your *own* team.

As you know, growing companies require people across teams, functions, departments, and recently acquired companies to learn to collaborate quickly. Cross-functional teams often form around a project or company goal, even though many of the individuals come from departments with competing priorities. These teams have the added challenge of being unaccustomed to working together. They have a limited amount of time to figure out how to work together, how to build trust, and how to make decisions. Cross-functional teams often disagree on what to do, are unsure of who does what by when, or gain little traction as projects stall for months. Communication is even more difficult post-acquisition when employees from an acquired company have to communicate with their new management team. As a result, hundreds of studies show that mergers and acquisitions fail to produce their expected value 50–80 percent of the time.

Usually, when we assess a company's culture, we see common areas of weakness.[1] Cross-functional collaboration and communication consistently receive the lowest scores, and interpersonal communication causes some of the greatest frustration. We find that an absence of clear direction and focus, weak or infrequent feedback, low motivation, and a lack of ownership of goals and accountability hamper a company's productivity and employee satisfaction.

When CEOs are presented with these results, they often push back. "Things are still good," they insist. "After all, doesn't every company have problems when people work together?"

Just because something is pervasive doesn't mean you should put up with it. If company-wide dysfunctions aren't addressed, they become insurmountable when the hardships of scale, fast-changing industries, evolving social systems, or increasing demands add to daily pressures. Think about the large number of once-innovative companies that have morphed into bureaucratic, stagnant cultures where significant parts of the workforce feel undervalued and ineffective.

Are you willing to accept this kind of mediocrity?

Lower-performing teams and an unmotivated workforce are a direct reflection of a company's leadership culture and how well the people in the company work together. While you may have great benefits, perks, and even a great set of values, the real test of a company's culture is how well people lead and work together when things get tough.

For this reason, a strong leadership culture is something a scaling company can't afford to be without. The problem is that most companies don't know how to create one. Deloitte surveyed over seven thousand global executives, and while 82 percent felt a strong culture is a competitive advantage, only 19 percent believe they have the "right culture."[2] Do you want to see how your team stacks up and what you can do to be a better team by Friday? There is a short version of our assessment in Appendix C, or visit *betterteam book.com* to take our complete assessment to see how your organization or team is performing.

WHAT TO DO ABOUT IT

Companies come to us because they've made the decision to reject mediocrity. You should, too. Even back in 1992, John Kotter and James Heskett found that companies with high-performance corporate cultures that adapt quickly to a changing world had a 756 percent increase in net profit over eleven years.[3] If the pandemic, distribution crises, and employee shortages indicate what's to come, the need for an adaptive leadership culture is far greater than it was decades ago. When your company and teams have the skills and tools that promote collaboration, you can achieve greatness, no matter what the outside world throws your way.

Your team won't develop those skills on their own. It doesn't matter if you hire the best and the brightest in your industry—becoming a high-performance team requires intentional effort. Management expert Peter Drucker says, "Only three things happen naturally in organizations: friction, confusion, and underperformance. Everything else requires leadership."[4] Sometimes the term "leadership" gets interpreted to mean "the person(s) in charge." But preventing the natural slide to underperformance Drucker warns about requires leadership from *everyone* on a team.

The first step is figuring out where you are. On a scale of 1 to 10, how high performing are your work teams? If a 1 is dismal and 10 is "we work so well together, Google is calling us to figure out what *we* are doing right," where are you?

Like many of our clients before they start working with us, you might choose a number somewhere between 4 and 7. Things are "pretty good," but you know there's room for improvement.

The gap between where you are now and a 10 represents your company's untapped potential. If people worked together so well that you could answer *emphatically*, "We are definitely a 10," what would be possible for you, your teams, and your company?

This book will help get you to 10 fast. As your team's playbook, *Be a Better Team by Friday* shows you how to create a shared leadership framework across your entire company. With a common set of practices, your teams will become highly skilled at working with each other—and across departments. Among other benefits, this framework ensures that team members become competent in the following skills:

☐ How to optimize cross-functional communication with a shared, company-wide style of communicating

☐ How to integrate company cultures post-acquisition, so engagement stays high (and attrition stays low)

☐ How to build a greater sense of purpose, passion, and fun across the company

☐ How to grow motivation and excitement on the team

☐ How to give tough feedback and have difficult conversations

☐ How to coach and develop each other, so everybody gets better every day

☐ How to get more done with less work

☐ How to delegate and build ownership

☐ How to lead effective, engaging meetings that advance the action

If you feel your company has untapped potential, intelligence, creativity, and innovation, what percentage do you think is offline?

Now, consider: What would happen if you could access even 10–20 percent more of your company's intelligence without hiring different people? That is the impact of these seven practices.

When applied, the practices in this book will cut through mediocrity and make you great. When teams and companies use these practices, personality conflicts dissolve. Trust builds. Communication improves among department teams and across functions. More focused work leads to faster results and greater productivity. Tensions ease, and team members start enjoying their work. Praise and appreciation replace criticism and blame.

When a CEO implements these practices company-wide, the culture changes. People describe the experience as "feeling like it did when we first started the company" or a "breath of fresh air." We also see a heightened sense of personal motivation. If the company has a lower employee Net Promoter Score (eNPS), which measures employee satisfaction, their score typically increases by thirty or forty points over the course of a year. If the company already has a high eNPS, the score continues to climb as long-standing communication problems, interpersonal tensions, and leadership issues fall away.

Most importantly, however, companies become adept at handling the immense pressures and stressors that growth brings. They also adapt quickly to the ever-changing world outside their door. As a result, bottom-line numbers often *wildly* surpass expectations.

In 2014, we began working with Four Hands, a global design and luxury goods manufacturing firm with factories in multiple countries. At the time, the company reported approximately $96 million in revenue.

Over five years, we taught the practices in this book to every executive, director, and manager in the company, who then introduced the techniques to their teams. By 2019, the company had grown to $194 million in revenue while increasing its gross margin from 27.9 percent to 34.7 percent.

In 2019, the United States government introduced 25 percent tariffs on Chinese merchandise with very little warning. With much of its manufacturing coming from China, the company needed to shift its operational structure in weeks. Using our high-performing team practices, their creativity, and their grit, they did it. It required teams across departments and continents to problem solve together. They communicated transparently to customers and asked vendors to find ways to become more efficient. They expanded sourcing from other countries, triple-sourced products, allocated products more quickly, and figured out how to strengthen their Chinese business.

Nine months later, the company had the highest revenue quarter in its history.

Then, after they successfully managed those economic restrictions, COVID-19 struck their factories in China and fractured their global supply chain. At the same time, the company was undergoing an overhaul of its operations software and a massive office renovation.

Despite these challenges, the company quickly adapted. All cross-functional heads met to identify the key challenges they had to work on together, and applied our tools to improve their collaborative communication. They pinpointed core focus areas and moved into coordinated action. Then they adapted on the fly.

They did all this while transitioning most of the organization to work from home and quickly implementing advanced COVID-19 protocols and technologies in their warehouses and factories.

Once again, they had their most successful quarter in company history. By the end of 2020, this company broke sales, shipping, and manufacturing records and ended the year just shy of the $270M revenue mark. They ended 2021 at $455M in revenue.

We've written this book for those of you who want to thrive like this, too. Maybe your company is performing reasonably well, but breakthrough, wild success feels out of reach. Or perhaps you're not satisfied with where you are now, and a high-performance culture is something you think you can only dream of. Within the pages of this book, we will show you that you *do* have the power to move the needle to higher performance. But it does take a willingness to do things differently than you're used to.

You've probably read a lot of business books that do a good job of describing the problems you're experiencing. Page after page, you recognize what's going on in your company. These books also offer a variety of suggestions for solving your problems, but too often, the solutions are more theoretical than practical. They don't actually tell you what to *do*.

This is not one of those books. The practices in these pages are meant to be applied "on the court." You can start using the techniques right away, in today's meetings. Consider this your playbook—a "how to"—for becoming a high-performance team.

Read it, and you'll know *exactly* what to do.

THIS BOOK IS FOR THE PEOPLE YOU CARE ABOUT

You've probably been on a high-performance team in the past. For some, it might have been a work team. For others, it was a high school or college sports team. Perhaps it was a fraternity or sorority project, a theater troupe, or a school club. Remember what it was like? People loved working together, they felt passionate, and there was an air of excitement whenever you got together. Maybe you experienced a sense of camaraderie so great it felt like family.

You want the teams you lead to feel like this, too. If you're anything like most of the managers we work with, you care a lot about the people on your teams. You want a sense of passion and excitement to show up in their work. You want them to go home to their families proud of their work and excited to come back the next day. You want to see the spark that happens when people love what they do.

Too often, that spark gets lost in the day-to-day tensions of a stressful work environment. Personality conflicts, lackluster meetings, and overwhelming to-do lists can wear down the most well-intentioned teams. Even if you *want* a high-performing team, you might not always know how to get it.

This book offers a set of clear practices that will inspire your teams to tap into their spark. The passion, excitement, pride, and energy that drive greatness will emerge. Work gets fun. Trust us; you'll love what happens.

The first step? Commit to the practices and begin. As Michael Jordan said: "If you try to shortcut the game, then the game will shortcut you. If you put forth the effort, good things will be bestowed upon you."[5]

HOW TO PARTICIPATE WITH THIS BOOK: BE A "LEARN-IT-ALL"

It would be easy to read *Be a Better Team by Friday* and compare it to books you've read in the past. You may think, "Oh, this is a lot like what _____ says in their book." Or you might think, "I already know this." You might even spend the whole time deciding whether you agree with us or not.

So, we're going to ask you to try something here.

Instead of thinking *Do I like this or not*, or *Do I agree with this or not?*, ask yourself: *In what ways is my team already practicing this? In what ways are we not? How could we apply this?*

Satya Nadella, the CEO of Microsoft, says, "Ultimately, the 'learn-it-all' will always do better than the 'know-it-all.'"[6] Commit to being a "learn-it-all" to avoid the trap of average performance. Stay creative and adaptive as you apply what you learn.

As you begin reading, you may quickly realize with alarming clarity that you are part of a lower-performing team (perhaps you already know this). Don't panic. We've witnessed, again and again, that when lower-performing teams commit to all the practices in this book, they become high-performing teams. We've never seen it fail.

Maybe your team is already high-performing, but you have no idea how much better you can be until you actively engage with all seven of these practices.

Stick with it!

HOW THIS BOOK IS STRUCTURED

Be a Better Team by Friday is a playbook for you to refer to on an ongoing basis. Each chapter is a practice. In each chapter, you will find *disciplines of the practice*, which are the basic exercises to apply repeatedly to build your skills.

For some people, words like "practice" and "discipline" bring up resistance, not unlike the word "diet." You know sticking with it consistently will give you the results you want, but you resist because it's difficult and uncomfortable.

If this describes you, keep in mind that the practices in this book aren't *hard* to apply. They just require a willingness on your team's part to think in new ways, try something different, and stick with it.

You'll notice that some words and phrases are in bold. Bolded and italicized words are intended to provide you with a shared language of high performance. When everyone on a team has a common language, it's easier to apply the practices as a team (or across teams). A complete list of those terms is in Appendix B.

Inside many of the disciplines, you will see questions to ask yourself and your teammates. These questions have been developed to facilitate better conversations. Asking great questions is more important to these practices than always having answers. We've provided questions to get you started, but you will also want to develop your own.

What do we recommend you do when you encounter one of these questions?

Pause.

> Consider a situation where the question might be relevant to you and your team. Reflect on your answers to each question. Ask yourself:
>
> ☐ How would I personally answer the question?
> ☐ How would my team members answer the question?

The insights you gain by asking yourself and others these questions are the starting point for applying the practices in your day-to-day work.

At the end of each chapter, you'll find structures for application to help you use the practices immediately. If you follow these recommended steps, you can be sure you are applying the practice in full.

MAKE THE CHOICE—AND THEN KEEP MAKING IT

Committing to being a learn-it-all is not a one-time thing. The truth is, you'll need to choose to embrace these practices every day. Over time, the practices will become an organic part of how your team communicates with one another—but you need to start by putting in the work.

If a particular practice sounds awkward or impossible, surrender your skepticism and just try it. We've found, again and again, that leaders are constantly surprised by the conversations these practices empower them and their teams to have. When they start working with us, their reactions are sometimes, "I'd *never* be able to say that," or, "My team would never be open to that." By the end, their communication skills are their superpower.

You're reading this book because you want your team to reach its full potential. The only way to do that is by trying things you've never tried before. Trust the process. Allow your team to surprise you. You might even surprise yourself.

ONE

CHOOSE YOUR MINDSET

"The most common way people give up their power is by thinking they don't have any."

—ALICE WALKER, writer

Being a great leader is not easy. In any job, at any organization, you will face challenges that at times seem insurmountable. You can't escape that fact even when you're on a team or in a company with a strong vision.

When you are a great leader, though, you move through hardship and accomplish goals despite the challenges. You choose to create a positive outcome, even when things get tough. You inspire others to be great, too.

How?

The first step to being a great leader is to *choose* to be great.

The next step is to empower your team to lead, too. Being a great leader does not mean you're a lone hero making all the decisions. Instead, it requires finding better ways to work together on your team when facing significant obstacles. Great leaders *work together* with their colleagues and direct reports to accomplish what they set out to do.

Gone are the days when "leadership" was assigned to a few people at the top of an org chart. In fast-changing times and fast-changing organizations, anyone with accountability to the company has a role in leading. To become more adaptive, agile, and effective in times of change, every individual on your team needs to *choose* greatness to *achieve* it despite all odds.

Everyone on high-performance teams chooses to excel. High-performance leadership mindsets enable high-performance collaboration. Team members choose an empowered way of thinking. As a result, they act in ways that move toward their goals while empowering others to accomplish theirs.

But before you can choose your way of thinking, you first must realize that *the way you think is a choice.*

YOUR MINDSET IS YOUR CHOICE

Imagine you're wearing orange-tinted glasses. If you were to look around the room, the room would look orange. Now, if you take the glasses off and put on a pair of green-tinted glasses, the room would appear green.

Your **mindset** is like those orange lenses, a filter through which you see the world. It is your way of thinking that leads to your way of acting. If you're thinking angry thoughts, you will act very differently than if you are thinking happy ones.

You might not even realize that the way you think *is* a mindset. It's like wearing the orange glasses but forgetting you have them on. You just think the world is orange. It's easy to forget that your way of thinking is only a mindset (orange!)—and that you can *choose* to change it.

Your mindset is the answer to the question:

☐ How am I thinking about this right now?

Two people in the same situation might have completely different mindsets and choose dramatically different responses. Someone frustrated with a meeting where nothing seems to get done might get visibly agitated and tell a colleague what a waste of time it is to attend the meeting. Another person decides to make the meeting better, captures action items, creates and circulates an agenda, keeps time, and makes a list of any off-topic agenda items.

The difference between these two people is their mindset about the exact same situation. The mindset of the first person leads him to be a spectator "in the spectator stands" watching and talking about the "game," but nothing changes—the meeting is still poor. The mindset of the second person gets her out of "the spectator stands" onto the "field of play," and it changes the game—the meeting gets better.

Likewise, to be a great leader, you have to choose the mindset of great leadership. To be a great team, everyone on the team has to choose the mindset of great teams. For this reason, we start this book with a piece of high-performance psychology: to *Be a Better Team by Friday*, you first have to *choose* to do it together.

As soon as you choose to do it, you're already better.

CHOOSE EMPOWERED MINDSETS

We live in a time that requires us all to adapt our ways of working together. Since March 2020, things have been in flux, and will continue to be so for the foreseeable future. We're not going to be able to do things the way we have in the past. As a society, we are all learning to adapt to fast-changing social, environmental, and health situations. And that's not going to slow down any time soon.

Your teams must choose to respond to changes with a mindset that's ready to adapt. To do this, you have to shift from a fixed mindset rooted in "how things have been done" to a growth mindset that asks, "How do we need to grow as a team to adapt?"

In *Mindset: The New Psychology of Success*, Stanford psychologist Carol Dweck describes a "fixed" mindset versus a "growth" mindset. A person with a fixed mindset is more likely to give up when they experience a challenge. A person with a growth mindset faces the same challenge and learns everything they can to overcome it.

Same situation, different mindset.

We know feedback is essential to growth. Everyone receives difficult feedback from time to time that's hard to hear. If someone has a fixed mindset, they'll hear this type of feedback as an indictment of their character or behavior. They might respond with all the reasons it's not true or not their fault. They go home and spend the evening arguing with the feedback in their head (or out loud with their spouse). "She doesn't know what she's talking about," they complain while secretly thinking, "I guess I'm just not good at my job, and now I have proof."

Professional athletes, elite performers, and those trained to choose a growth mindset receive the same feedback but respond differently. At first, it might sting—difficult feedback is hard for anyone to take. But instead of defending themselves, they think:

Okay, that's disappointing to hear. Maybe I don't agree with all of it.

But what can I learn from this?

How can I use it to improve?

They're continuously willing to take feedback into account, and their performance improves—often significantly—as a result.

Basically, they grow.

A growth mindset is an example of an **empowered mindset**. People with an empowered mindset think in such a way that it leads them to take powerful actions. People with empowered mindsets move toward what they want, even in the face of adversity. Great leaders practice coming back to an empowered mindset again and again and again. This empowered mindset sets the stage to accelerate peak-team performance.

A fixed mindset is an example of a **disempowered mindset**. Disempowered mindsets lead to disempowered actions. Someone with a disempowered mindset will feel helpless to change a situation.

We worked with a team that discovered that a client planning to invest a large sum toward new product development was backing out. The news was devastating, and everyone on the team naturally felt deeply disappointed. It was a tough afternoon. But the team had the marks of high performance. They turned the situation around in one day, helping each other shift to see new options. They asked each other questions like:

"What other options do we have?"

"Knowing what we know now, what could we do differently?"

"What happened has happened. Now, what's next?"

The team reached out to their network, and soon their director was on the phone with three new potential investors. They had to do some significant redesigns, but eventually found a funding partner that made a *larger* investment than what they had lined up in the first place. Their empowered mindsets inspired them to act in ways that produced phenomenal results despite a tremendous setback.

What might that same situation have looked like on a lower-performing team? Finger-pointing, complaining, and "it wasn't my fault." Maybe they would blame the investors—or each other. They see the situation as a series of problems and figure, "There's no way out of this. Why try?" They give up.

And if even *one person* on your team has a disempowered mindset, your entire team's ability to collaborate will be compromised. A study on group behavior found that one "bad apple" on the team can bring team productivity down 30 to 40 percent. In other words, negativity is contagious.[7]

OVERCOME THE NEGATIVITY BIAS

Humans are hardwired to complain. Perhaps you have noticed that it's easier to focus on what's wrong than on what's going well. This is due to a phenomenon called the **negativity bias**. In their book, *The Power of Bad*, John Tierney and Roy F. Baumeister define this bias as the "universal tendency for negative events and emotions to affect us more strongly than positive ones."[8] While we might think we are being objective, our brains are often *biased* toward seeing the negative.

Imagine you have a day where things are going your way. All day long, people compliment you on your work, your ideas, and even on how good you look. You lead a great meeting and make tremendous strides on a project you've been working on for months. But right before the end of the day, you have a last-minute conversation with your boss, who shares that a client is unhappy with your work from a few weeks ago. That night after work, what do you go home thinking about? For most people, that last piece of bad news overshadows the day's positive events.

The tendency to focus on what's wrong is programmed into the more primal regions of our brains. It's a survival strategy. There's a tiny part of your brain called the amygdala dedicated to ensuring you're safe from harm. The amygdala is on the lookout for anything that could go wrong. Our primitive ancestors survived because they could stay vigilant enough to avoid physical threats in dangerous environments. If we keep our eyes out for tigers, we can get out of the way before they eat us.

Most corporate employees are not surrounded by tigers, but our brains are still at work, on the lookout for danger. There are advantages to seeing potential threats in the workplace, but not at the expense of slanting our bias toward the negative. A bias is not an accurate perception, which is why it's called a bias! This negativity bias tells us that things are much worse than they are.

When a team leader has too much negativity bias, the team that works for them will, too. One executive we worked with consistently complained about his company's problems, and everything he feared would go wrong in the future. The situation sounded so dire that we asked him, "Do you think your company will fail?" He looked a bit shocked and said, "Oh, not at all. In fact, this was the best year in the history of the company."

Unfortunately, he brought this negativity bias into his team meetings. Because he spent so much time and energy pointing out everything that was wrong and *could* go wrong, his team thought things were terrible. Their meetings were unfocused and fueled by stress. They were operating under an immense sense of unnecessary pressure. They made reactive decisions to avoid bad things happening instead of proactively working toward a shared vision.

We suggested he focus time during every meeting to discuss what he saw was going well. This small shift away from the negativity bias led to immediate improvement of team morale. With more focus on their accomplishments, the stress and worry were reduced. As a result, decisions they made focused more on working toward their goals and less on "fighting the fires" of constant dread and concern. It's incredible how such a simple switch can produce immediate results.

YOUR MINDSET—AND THESE PRACTICES— WILL GET YOU THROUGH

Escaping the trap of the negativity bias requires choosing a different mindset about the situation. The most important aspect of a mindset is that *a mindset is something you choose*. While circumstances might be out of your control, how you think about your situation is always a choice.

Of course, choosing an empowered mindset doesn't mean your challenges go away. Negativity bias will still creep up, too, because you're human. The difference is that when you have the self-awareness to Choose Your Mindset, you can get out of your own way faster.

When COVID-19 hit, one company we worked with saw their entire industry shut down overnight. They had only a few months of cash left, and prospective investors started doubting whether their product had viability during a pandemic. It almost seemed inevitable: they could have easily folded, and few would have questioned that choice.

But they didn't. They chose to reinvent themselves and their product—fast. Within ninety days, they secured a new, top-tier lead investor, and six months later they had designs for a new product in a new industry. The executive team was determined to find a solution, even when the odds were against them. Talk about an empowered mindset! Had *anyone* on this team succumbed to their negativity bias with a disempowered mindset—complaining, pointing fingers, giving up—they could not have orchestrated such a speedy turnaround.

On lower-performing teams, the weeds of disempowered mindsets—particularly at the executive level—make it difficult to regain equilibrium in a crisis. Even if a company is financially stable and experiencing a reasonable degree of success, high yields in a strong market often mask inefficiency and lead to an infectious, company-wide complacency. When tough times arise (and they will), the fragile infrastructure becomes exposed, and things fall apart.

On high-performing teams, everyone on the team challenges their negativity biases. These team members rarely complain or judge each other poorly. They deal with the tough stuff by taking a moment to absorb the upset and moving quickly into finding solutions. They are direct with each other and ask for what they need. They coach and challenge each other to be better. Team members think positively about their teammates, which reinforces a different set of behaviors and outcomes. Because they see the strengths in the people they work with, they act in a way that empowers each other.

Now, to be clear, simply *deciding* to have an empowered mindset won't get you to a place where you can achieve all these things. You'll need to embrace every practice in this book to build the trust, communication skills, work style, and motivation needed to tackle problems in such a proactive and collaborative way.

But you can't do any of it without first choosing an empowered mindset.

You can even notice while you read this book: Are you in an empowered mindset right now? Or are you reading this with a negativity bias?

The choice is yours!

(Of course, we encourage you to choose to read with an empowered mindset.)

CHOOSE IN EVERY MOMENT

Keep in mind that your mindset is ever-changing. On average, you think at least six thousand thoughts a day.[9] The way you think is always in flux. It's natural and normal to slip into the negativity bias from time to time.

Great leaders don't think, "Oh, I learned about mindsets before. I always have an empowered mindset." Instead, they practice self-awareness and choose their mindset in every moment.

In the book *The Mental Game of Baseball* by H. A. Dorfman, sports psychologist Michael Maloney notes, "The difference between two athletes is 20% physical and 80% mental."[10] A golfer notices and chooses her mindset every single step on the golf course and makes constant adjustments to stay empowered to win. She will even have mindset coaches to help her do it, using music and physical cues and often following highly structured preparation rituals to get in the right mindset before the game. When Olympic athletes have headphones in before the race, they prepare and maintain a certain mindset. Baseball Hall of Famers Hank Aaron and Wade Boggs would practice visualizing hitting the ball to get into an empowered state before stepping up to the plate. Boxer Muhammad Ali famously repeated, "I am the greatest," and became it.

For the highest performers, a mindset is not one and done. Many leaders do not realize that, just like with great athletes, moment-to-moment mindset awareness and choice are equally essential in work as in sports. To be great at work, you Choose Your Mindset in every moment.

Most importantly, in any circumstance, you remember that you *always* have a choice to change the way you think.

WE *ALL* NEED TO GET OUT OF OUR OWN WAY

Your mindset is the foundation that your entire leadership operating system relies on. So, before we get to the rest of the practices, here is a set of tools to help you and your team stay aware of your mindset at all times—so you can change it when you need to.

Many executives make the mistake of thinking that once they learn how to choose an empowered mindset, they'll never be in a disempowered mindset again. It doesn't work that way. Even the best performers will fall into victim mode sometimes. We're basically in a disempowered mindset whenever we feel frustrated, and we need to do the work of pulling ourselves out of it. But the longer you do this, the quicker you'll be able to recognize your mindset and change your lens.

As a leader, it's important to be aware of this common oversight. Many executives believe that choosing your mindset is a task *everyone else* on their team needs to do, not them. Nobody is excused from putting in this work, including you!

Life and work are difficult, and it's normal to feel disempowered sometimes. But what distinguishes the high-performing teams from their lower-performing counterparts is that every member—at every level—supports each other, again and again, to return to empowered mindsets regardless of the circumstances.

The practice of choosing an empowered mindset is a simple one, but it requires tremendous effort. For this reason, we recommend that teams commit to the discipline as a group for shared accountability. The following three steps will help your team shift from a disempowered mindset to an empowered one:

1. Realize you are in a disempowered mindset.
2. Choose an empowered mindset.
3. Coach each other to choose empowered mindsets.

1. Realize You Are In a Disempowered Mindset

The first step in choosing an empowered mindset is recognizing you are in a disempowered mindset in the first place. Another term for this is **self-awareness**. Often, when you are stuck in a disempowered mindset, you don't realize it.

Imagine you're sitting on a stopped highway complaining about traffic. You say to yourself, "There are too many cars on the road. This city is growing too fast." You have a whole conversation about it in your head. Meanwhile, your spouse is sitting beside you, perfectly content, thinking about what to order for dinner at the restaurant you're going to.

The traffic is not irritating *everyone*. How you're *thinking* about the traffic is irritating you. The orange-colored glasses you're wearing are usually unconscious at first. You don't realize in the moment that how you are thinking is a choice. You think that's just the way things are. (Idiot drivers, lousy roads, etc.) The choice, however, is as simple as asking yourself:

☐ How could I think differently about this situation?

Knowing that you *can* choose a different way of thinking is critical. But you have to want to. Sometimes, venting might feel good. Maybe you'd rather feel the pleasure of complaining than do the hard work of choosing a different mindset. But how good does complaining *really* feel in the long run? It's important to realize that, while you can complain all you want if it helps you blow off steam, you still have a choice. If you wanted to think differently, you could.

Choosing a different mindset is always up to you. It's the one thing that no one and no situation can take away from you: the way you think is entirely up to you. It's what Holocaust survivor and psychologist Viktor Frankl points to in his book *Man's Search for Meaning*: "Everything can be taken from a man but one thing: the last of the human freedoms—to choose one's attitude in any given set of circumstances, to choose one's own way."[11]

When your disempowered mindset *is* unconscious, though, you need the people around you to point it out. When someone you work with skillfully points out your mindset, you can choose a different way of thinking. That's why high-performing teammates help each other grow in self-awareness like great coaches. They can help you see your blind spots—if you're willing to let them.

The work of psychiatrist Stephen Karpman, MD, provides the most useful model we've found to help teams work with their mindsets. He called his model the "drama triangle."[12] Regarding interpersonal dysfunction, people usually exhibit one of three dis-empowered behaviors: complaining, rescuing, and blaming. (Note: In Karpman's work, he refers to these three as specific roles people play: the "victim," the "rescuer," and the "persecutor." We find it helpful to speak about the particular behaviors someone exhibits versus the role someone plays.)

DISEMPOWERED MINDSETS

Complaining (Victim)
Helpless; Nothing can be done;
"Here's what's wrong with that."

Rescuing (Rescuer)
Sees others as helpless;
Does everything themselves;
"I will just do it myself."

Blaming (Persecutor)
Tears down others;
"Who is at fault?"

If an individual or team is stuck in a **complaining mindset**, they whine a lot. They see themselves as victims of their situation. They think they're powerless to do anything about it, so they talk (a lot) about their problems. They campaign aggressively to justify their points of view, trying to convince others that the situation is hopeless and there's "nothing we can do about it." They say things like, "The problem with that is...", "Yeah but...", and "That can't work because..."

A person stuck in a complaining mindset doesn't cope well with conflict. He wants to be saved or rescued from his problems. When he complains, he's grasping onto someone or something to make himself feel better. He hopes his teammates will validate his point by saying something like, "I see what you mean. That *is* terrible." Sometimes if a person isn't available, he looks to be rescued by things like TV, food, alcohol, or shopping to make himself feel better. As you can imagine, a complaining mindset can be extremely toxic to a team.

If an individual or team is stuck in the **rescuer mindset**, she tries to fix everyone else's problems. A person in this mindset is seen as a helper, and usually doesn't realize this is a disempowered mindset. It *seems* at first like a good thing to be a rescuer. But by doing everything for everybody else, she doesn't empower others to be resourceful (and takes on the burden of a lot of extra work). She can't stand to see others suffer, so she "rescues" them from the discomfort of challenge or failure. She usually thinks her own way of doing something is the "right" way. She often says, "If I don't do it, it won't get done," or, "I'll just do it." She's swamped because she's rescuing everybody else. Rescuers often have people come to them repeatedly with their difficulties, unloading complaints—and problems—on the rescuer. Sometimes a person with a rescuing mindset even quietly resents those they help, thinking, "Why do I have to do everything?"

If an individual or team is stuck in the **blaming mindset**, they continually find fault in others. A person with a blaming mindset harshly judges others' ideas, talents, or contributions. When he receives feedback, he says things like, "I would have done that but..." and makes excuses about why it's not his fault. He continually accuses others of being wrong by making all-encompassing statements like, "They *always (or never)*..." or, "If I worked with smarter or more competent people, I could..." Those with a blaming mindset tear down other people and work hard to get the rest of the team to agree. At their worst, people with habitually blaming mindsets can be intimidating or bullying.

Here is an example of these three mindsets in action:

Johnny, a mid-level developer, has been working on a project with Sharon, the Chief Product Officer. This is the first time he has worked with an executive in the company, and it's not going as well as he hoped. One day, Sharon lets Johnny know she will replace him on the project if he doesn't pick up the pace. She also suggests he take an additional training course if he wants to advance at the company.

Johnny leaves the meeting crushed. He finds his teammate, Steve, in the hallway and tells him what happened, ending with, "You know, I'm sick of this company. The leadership here is awful. This place used to be great, but it's not like it was two years ago."

His teammate nods and says, "Sharon, has no idea what she's talking about. All she does is make more demands. I see it all the time. You don't need more training. You're one of the best we've got. You're right; I remember back when it was more creative around here. It's too process-driven now. I miss the old days, but what can you do?"

They spend a few more minutes discussing the problems and then return to work. Johnny feels a bit better until he meets with Sharon the next time.

In this case, Johnny has a complaining mindset. He complains to Steve, who immediately takes a rescuer mindset—rescuing Johnny from feeling bad by agreeing with him. They are *both* in a blaming mindset when they blame the company's leadership for the deterioration of the culture. Nothing gets done to change anything, but they do feel a little better for a while.

Until Johnny realizes he's stuck in a disempowered mindset, he'll continue to feel powerless at his job. It's a self-fulfilling prophecy: he believes he's powerless, so he acts in a way that reflects this belief. He stays stuck. But what will it take for him to get out of his disempowered mindset? First, the self-awareness that he is in a disempowered mindset. Then, the knowledge of what a different, more empowered mindset would look like. And finally, he must choose the empowered mindset.

You can use the language of disempowered mindsets to help you identify when you're stuck. As long as the thoughts in your mind are complaining about something or someone, thinking about everyone else's problems, or making negative judgments about people, you can be sure you are in a disempowered mindset. Usually, we don't realize when we're stuck in a mindset. By adopting a shared language around disempowered mindsets, team members can more easily help one another by pointing out when we have slipped into one.

2. Choose the Empowered Mindset

The good news is, for each disempowered mindset, there is a counter empowered mindset to choose from. In his book *The Power of* TED* (*The Empowerment Dynamic*), David Emerald identifies three empowerment mindsets to choose whenever you get stuck in a disempowered mindset. He calls these the *creator*, the *coach*, and the *challenger*.[13]

Here is a map of these mindsets to support your application of this practice:

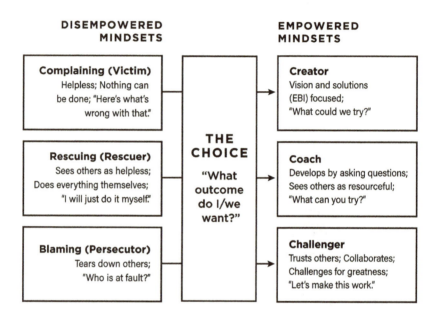

DISEMPOWERED MINDSETS		EMPOWERED MINDSETS
Complaining (Victim) Helpless; Nothing can be done; "Here's what's wrong with that."	**THE CHOICE** "What outcome do I/we want?"	**Creator** Vision and solutions (EBI) focused; "What could we try?"
Rescuing (Rescuer) Sees others as helpless; Does everything themselves; "I will just do it myself."		**Coach** Develops by asking questions; Sees others as resourceful; "What can you try?"
Blaming (Persecutor) Tears down others; "Who is at fault?"		**Challenger** Trusts others; Collaborates; Challenges for greatness; "Let's make this work."

We show you exactly how to do all the action items mentioned in our breakdown of empowered mindsets below. Each tool in the chapters ahead teaches you how to listen, ask for help, give feedback, and adjust your work style so you can experience similar—and pretty immediate—transformations in your team.

From Complaining → Creator

In her book of essays, *Wouldn't Take Nothing for My Journey Now*, Maya Angelou recounts a piece of advice that her grandmother gave her as a small child: "What you're supposed to do when you don't like a thing is change it. If you can't change it, change the way you think about it. Don't complain."[14]

Her grandmother's wisdom is at the heart of this discipline.

The complaining mindset keeps you stuck talking about what's wrong without doing anything about it, but a **creator mindset** asks:

- ☐ What is the specific outcome I/we want?
- ☐ What could we try to get there?

High-performing individuals or teams choosing an empowered mindset understand that difficult stuff happens all the time. Instead of complaining, you move quickly into action to make something better happen. You focus on the outcome you want versus getting stuck talking in circles about how bad things are.

One team manager we worked with frequently came to his coaching sessions with a cloud over his head. Week after week, he reported nothing but complaints. "Everything I try doesn't work. The problem is the executive team, and my boss specifically." Then he would give us a lot of reasons why he was never going to make any progress at his company.

At one session, we asked him to review the empowered mindsets model. "Looking at this, which mindset are you coming from?" He looked at the model for a long time and grew a bit sheepish as self-awareness dawned on him. "I guess I've been in the complaining mindset, haven't I?"

We asked, "What do you want in this situation?"

He told us he really wanted a relationship with his boss like he had at his old company. He wanted a sense of partnership and mentorship. He missed that and found it challenging to work with his current boss. We asked him for one suggestion on how he might build that kind of relationship with his boss. He thought for a moment and said, "You know, I've never actually asked for what I want from her. Maybe I could start by asking for a bit more guidance."

He did just that, asking her, specifically, for more mentorship. Over the next six months, he set up a bi-weekly meeting with her, coming to each session with specific questions. As time went on, trust between them grew. Not only had she become a mentor, but their collaboration improved. She began to come to him with questions as well. Because he continued to take actions from a creator mindset, his relationship with his boss improved significantly.

From Rescuing → Coach

Where the rescuing mindset tells you to fix everyone else's problems, the **coach mindset** has you thinking about ways to support others to fix their own problems. Instead of jumping in and doing everything *for* them, you prioritize developing others' capacity to find solutions for themselves. An individual or team that chooses a coach mindset assumes that everyone is growing every day. They see challenges as opportunities for growth. Instead of rescuing, trying to fix the problem by giving advice, or doing it themselves, they coach each other by asking questions like:

- ☐ What do you think are some potential solutions?
- ☐ What have you tried?
- ☐ What could you try?
- ☐ What will you do differently?

One manager we worked with had a phenomenal capacity for doing a significant amount of work—60 to 80 hours a week. But she was near burnout. After learning about the rescuer mindset, she had an epiphany. She realized she was doing other people's work for them. She wanted to be helpful by not overloading them with work. She tried to rescue people from having too much to do but ended up overly stressed herself without any time for a personal life.

As this manager became more aware of her mindset, she began delegating projects to her team and developing their capacity to complete them. She spent a lot of time early on training them and then became more hands-off, serving as their coach and mentor. When they came to her with problems, she asked them how they would solve the issue instead of fixing it herself.

To her surprise, over time, her teammates started asking for extra work; they loved having more responsibility! Some weeks she delegated up to 80 percent of the work she had been doing, freeing her up to think more strategically about the team's next six months and easing the stress she had taken on. She also used some of the spare time to take a regular yoga class she had always put off because she's been "too busy."

From Blaming → Challenger

Where the blaming mindset makes everyone else wrong, the **challenger mindset** figures out how to work together to address the challenge. A challenger stands shoulder to shoulder with you, demanding you to bring all the greatness you have forward. Individuals and teams who choose a challenger mindset believe every obstacle can be overcome. It's not always easy, but they challenge each other to be better and solve problems. Instead of blaming, they believe in others' capabilities and help each other achieve. They see greatness and potential in others and celebrate their success.

We often hear examples of great bosses being tough but supportive. We hear things like, "The best boss I ever had wasn't always easy to work with, but she always saw that I had more potential than I saw in myself. She challenged me to be great, and I grew more working with her than in my whole career." That's what a challenger mindset brings.

The challenger mindset asks questions like:

☐ "What would you do if you could not fail?"
☐ "What do you need to be great?"
☐ "What specific actions will you take?"

One manager we worked with liked to say, "You can't fix stupid." He believed he worked with incompetent people, which he mentioned a lot. In meetings, he'd blame his team's mediocre results on their lack of effort. When we asked what he was doing about it, he said, "I've given up trying. My team members are too lazy to want to do anything."

When we first introduced him to the disempowered mindset, he had a hard time seeing himself as a blamer. But when we asked, "If your job is, first and foremost, to make sure your team excels, how are you getting in the way of your team's performance? In what ways are you not living up to your end of the bargain?" This was tough for him to hear, but eventually, he admitted he saw his team's lack of effort as a personal failure. He was up for trying something different. He also admitted something else: he felt uncomfortable pushing his team harder. He didn't want to deal with their complaints. Ultimately, he thought it would get worse if he pushed too hard.

The first thing we asked him to do was to identify what his team members did well. Then we asked him to identify what specific areas of performance he wanted to see improve. He met with each individual and gave specific feedback about what they did well and where they needed to step up. He told them he believed they could do it, even though it would be hard. He asked, "What do you need from me to do this well?" He also identified specifically what he could hold each of them accountable for—and let them know he'd support them along the way.

What this manager learned shaped his thinking. By having one-on-one conversations with each person on his team, he began to rebuild the trust he'd lost over months of blaming them for their lack of effort. He saw new ways to support each team member, challenging them to get better results. As outcomes started to improve, he realized the team had much more competence and capability than he had previously acknowledged. It took a shift in **mindset** from blaming to challenging to see it. It had been easier for him to blame everyone for their laziness rather than push for greatness. This shift required his willingness to take on the role of challenger, pushing his teammates in a way that supported their growth.

3. Coach Each Other to Choose Empowered Mindsets

Even on high-performing teams, every single person will get stuck in disempowered mindsets from time to time. We are all human beings, and we are all dealing with immense challenges. It's normal (and sometimes necessary) to get upset by things. But high-performing teams are different from other teams because they help each other choose empowering mindsets. They coach each other to return to an empowered mindset, especially in the face of adversity.

Let's revisit the story of Johnny (the guy complaining about Sharon to his coworker, Steve) and his complaining mindset from earlier in this chapter. The day after complaining to Steve, Johnny goes to his manager, Isabel, with the exact same complaint. "Sharon doesn't know what she wants and has no idea how hard I'm working. I don't see how I can win with her."

Isabel has an option here. Immediately, she thinks, "I really don't need Sharon deflating my team members. We don't have time for this. I'll talk to her tomorrow and take care of it." But she catches herself: if she fixes Johnny's problem for him, that's a rescuer mindset. She wants to empower her team, not rescue them.

Instead, she asks if he's up for some coaching around the situation, which he agrees to. She practices deep listening and makes sure she understands Johnny's full perspective. Then she shows Johnny the chart of the disempowered and empowered mindsets, asking, "Which mindset are you in right now?"

Johnny doesn't love admitting it, but he can see he's been in the complaining mindset. Isabel asks him, "What are some outcomes you might want in this situation?"

"I want to deliver a great product, and I want Sharon to recognize I can do it."

Isabel continues, "What are some options you might try to get there?"

Johnny thinks about it briefly. "Well, Sharon suggested I take an additional training course. But what good would that do? She's just going to find more problems with my work."

At this point, Isabel challenges Johnny, "It sounds like you don't think there's anything you can do. But you're talented and have the capability to do great work. If you *could* prove this to Sharon, what might be some ways you can get her to see this?"

Johnny thought about it. He acknowledged additional training could be useful. He added that he didn't always communicate with Sharon about the work he was doing. It was going to be a stretch for him, but he agreed to schedule a weekly meeting with Sharon for the next four weeks to get her input on his work. Instead of giving up and complaining about it, he chose to take action that, while challenging, could get him on track.

By the time the project was done, Johnny and Sharon had developed such a great working relationship that Sharon began requesting him as the developer on her future projects. She knew she could trust him to get the work done thoughtfully and on time, and that he'd step up to problem solve if they ran into hurdles along the way. Johnny was promoted to senior developer shortly after he and Sharon began their third project together. He also took on a leadership role in his department, training junior developers to work better with executives (using many of the tools in this book). *And* Johnny shared with us that Sharon became one of the most important mentors in his life.

> Here is a simple structure for coaching someone like Isabel did for Johnny. You can use this structure to support your colleagues to help them shift from disempowered to empowered mindsets:
>
> **Step 1**, ask questions:
>
> 1. Ask them to explain their frustration to you.
> 2. Practice deep listening. Make sure they acknowledge you understand their situation exactly. (We cover deep listening in the next chapter.)
> 3. Ask: Are you up for some coaching on this?

4. Show them the Empowerment Mindsets grid.
5. Ask: Which mindset would you say you are in right now?
6. Ask: What is the best-case outcome you want in this situation?
7. Ask: What are some specific actions that could help you move toward that outcome?
8. Ask: What, exactly, will you do?

Step 2: Practice deep listening, is critical here. It may be hard to resist jumping in and offering your solution to a problem right away, but rescuing is not coaching. Instead, encourage your colleagues to return to empowerment mindsets and find solutions for themselves. You might be surprised at how people are more resourceful at finding answers for themselves than you could ever be, even if you think you know best.

THE ONE QUESTION TO REMEMBER

At the heart of this practice of choosing your mindset is an understanding that your mindset is always your choice, no matter the circumstance. Sure, it's hard to do, and it requires admitting that you can take responsibility for your situation. When you choose a new mindset, though, you see new solutions. When you make this choice, you have the power to change your circumstances.

This choice always comes down to one simple question:

"In this situation, what is the outcome I/you/we want, and what can I/you/we do about it?"

Start there.

CHOOSE YOUR MINDSET

STRUCTURE FOR APPLICATION

1. Practice, as a team, pointing out your tendency to move into a negativity bias. Ask, "What is also going well that we can focus on?"

2. Teach the matrix of disempowered versus empowered mindsets to all team members and get permission from each team member to coach each other.

3. Throughout the week, practice identifying any time your thoughts go into complaining about something, thinking about fixing someone else's problem, or blaming someone. Ask yourself, "Am I in a disempowered mindset right now?"

4. Any time you or someone on your team is in a disempowered mindset:
   - ☐ *See* the choice you/they have by identifying which mindset you/they are in.
   - ☐ Ask, "Do I/you want to choose a different mindset?"
   - ☐ Help yourself/them choose a different mindset by asking, "What outcome do I/you want in this situation?"
   - ☐ Ask, "What are some options for moving forward in that direction?"

TWO

GET REAL WITH EACH OTHER

"I only wish I could find an institute that teaches people how to listen. Business people need to listen at least as much as they need to talk. Too many people fail to realize that real communication goes in both directions."

—LEE IACOCCA, former president and CEO, Chrysler Corporation

In fast-growth companies, things change so quickly that the teams you worked with a year ago might look a lot different today. Market shifts, re-orgs, mergers and acquisitions, cross-department projects, and people coming and going demand the ability to adapt quickly. High-performance teams that do this well have high trust. They have open, honest conversations. They're direct, empathetic, and vulnerable with each other. They listen deeply, and debate without dissolving into argument. These are the teams where hard things come up, and they can say what is needed to work together and still get the desired results. They Get Real with Each Other and trust that everyone on the team has their back.

Teams build trust when they approach leadership as a conversation. Whether you're in a meeting, on emails, on Slack, on Zoom, in the finance books, or on a sales call, you're managing many different conversations. Regardless of your role in the company, how well you lead depends on how well you manage many conversations. But a conversation is not just what you say. It's also, more importantly, what you hear. When you listen well, you listen to understand what someone else is communicating.

But many leaders (and people in general) have a huge blind spot when speaking with others: they don't realize that *how we listen* is a choice, much like they don't consider that our **mindset** is a choice. So they talk a lot and get in more disputes, tension ensues, and the wheels keep spinning without much movement.

When you see leadership as a conversation, it's alarming to think that most of us are oblivious to 50 percent of the interaction. It's such a prevalent problem because listening is a skill most of us haven't spent much time developing. When was the last time you took a class on listening? Unless you've taken leadership training, maybe never. Most of us learn a lot about speaking and writing, but few people make a concerted effort to develop the skill of listening.

Listening underlies the heart of the other practices in this book. If you talk more than you listen, you may have room to grow your listening skills. As Robert Greenleaf says in *Servant Leadership*, "Don't assume because you are intelligent, able, and well-motivated, that you are open to communication, that you know how to listen."[15]

When you practice deep listening, you empower your team-mates to get real with you. You foster the trust that allows them to be honest and vulnerable. Once that trust is in place, you might be surprised to hear what the people on your team *really* think.

When we start working with executive teams, we interview each team member one-on-one. We get the unique opportunity to hear what they *don't* say in meetings. They share their doubts, frustrations, and lack of confidence in other team members. Most of the time, each team member has a completely different point of view about what's wrong.

We ask, "Have you shared these thoughts with your team?"

The answer is almost always, "There is no way I could say all this."

When we present aggregated comments to the CEO, we'll often hear, "I knew some of this, but I had no idea it was *this* bad. Sure, we have weak spots, but I thought we had a good rapport. I'm surprised I was so far off."

On a scale of 1 to 10, how open and honest do you think your team is with each other?

If you can't confidently answer a 9 or 10, then people are holding back. If they're holding back, you can be assured frustrations are building. As a result, your team's performance is not where it could be.

HIGH TRUST = HIGH PERFORMANCE

Over the course of two years, Google's Aristotle Project studied 180 teams to determine the factors of team high performance. They concluded that the *single most important* determinant of a team's performance is **psychological safety**.[16] High-performing team members trust and respect each other and speak freely about concerns, ideas, and mistakes without fearing negative consequences. Lower-performing teams don't.

If you think back to the highest-performing team you have ever been on—a work team, a sports team, or a project team—you probably experienced a high degree of psychological safety. You might describe the experience like this: "We could say anything to each other," or, "We all knew we had each other's backs," or, "It felt like a family."

High-performance teams almost always have that level of trust and camaraderie. When we sit at the table with a high-performing team, we see a lot of respect among everyone. When one person speaks, the others listen. Team members have *real* conversations—in person—about topics that are hard to broach. Each person considers points of view that conflict with their own. They deliberate and make decisions collectively, without arguing all the time.

Teams with low psychological safety have a different dynamic. People are polite and professional. They might even go out to happy hour with each other occasionally, but everybody knows that some people on the team don't get along. In meetings, one or two people have particularly dominant voices, talking much more than everyone else. Decisions are rarely a consensus. Conversations turn into circular arguments, with the same opinions voiced repeatedly. The less-vocal team members find it easier to say nothing. Sometimes, people describe it as a feeling: meetings are always tense; they dread going to them. Because honest conversations don't happen, resentments and frustration turn into off-the-record gossip. Negativity increases, engagement decreases.

Quite often, this dynamic gets heightened on cross-functional teams, when members from different departments come together over a shared task. They've often come to the table with significantly competing priorities. For instance, an engineering team, a sales team, and an operational team all have different agendas. What might seem like a good idea to the sales team, e.g., selling an unfinished product to a new client, could seem detrimental to the capacity in engineering. The engineers say, "Why are you selling what we can't offer?" The sales team says, "Why aren't you moving faster and accommodating what our customers want?" The operational team says, "We're stretched to deliver as it is. How can you expect us to keep up with the new offer?" These conflicting points of view heighten tension, resulting in meetings that feel more like high-stakes negotiations than collaboration. Psychological safety is low, communication falters, and everyone returns to their respective departments complaining about the "other side."

Sometimes, the issue points directly to the person in charge. We once worked with a team where psychological safety was particularly low. The team manager regularly dismissed others who disagreed with him. An outspoken team member told us, "I'm getting fed up. I talk with everyone individually, and they tell me they're frustrated with the guy. We form a plan to bring this up at the next meeting, but when we get there, nobody but me says anything. I end up being the bad guy, arguing with our boss. Everybody else suddenly starts acting like there's nothing wrong."

While the symptoms of low psychological safety might vary from team to team, one thing is for sure: with low psychological safety comes low trust. Without trust, your team won't perform at optimal levels. During times of heightened stress, the constant undercurrent of tension on your team will only exacerbate. This is one reason author Simon Sinek found that Navy SEAL Team 6, considered the best of the best, ranks trust even higher than individual performance. The SEALS concluded that a medium performer with high trust makes the team better than a high performer with medium trust. When the going gets tough, trust in the team outweighs the ability to perform a duty.[17]

So, how do you build psychological safety on teams that don't have it? By listening. Teams with a high degree of psychological safety *listen* to each other. Teams with low psychological safety don't. Psychological safety disappears when people don't feel heard or sense that speaking up is not safe. Google's Aristotle Project revealed that when psychological safety is high, "teammates feel safe to take risks around their team members. They feel confident that no team member will embarrass or punish anyone else for admitting a mistake, asking a question, or offering a new idea."

That's why **deep listening** is critical to achieving peak performance. It's a high-skill form of listening that deepens connection and encourages direct and honest communication. When teams listen to each other, psychological safety goes up, which in turn builds trust.

BUILD YOUR TEAM'S LISTENING MUSCLE

Deep listening is mandatory for creating a safe space for people to Get Real with Each Other. It also lays a foundation for significantly better communication. Have you ever had the experience where someone repeats exactly what you just said, and you think, "Didn't I already say that?" Or, you seem to talk about the same thing every time your team meets, almost as if the last meeting had never happened? Usually, this points to an issue with poor communication on your team.

Poor communication is costing your company money, time, and productivity. A 2014 study published by Siemens Enterprise Communications found that "a business with 100 employees spends an average downtime of 17 hours a week clarifying communications, translating to an annual cost of \$528,443."[18] The Economist Intelligence Unit 2018 Study of 403 executives, managers, and employees in the US found that "communication barriers are leading to a delay or failure to complete projects (44%), low morale (31%), missed performance goals (25%) and even lost sales (18%)—some worth hundreds of thousands of dollars."[19]

An inability to communicate is like the old saying, "If a tree falls in the woods and no one is around to hear it, does it make a sound?" No matter how well you speak (or how loudly), if your message isn't *heard and understood*, then communication doesn't really happen. When everyone on a team knows how to *listen* well, these communication issues dissipate. Frustrations, conflicts, tensions, and even cross-functional silos begin to dissolve. Project goals are achieved. Morale improves.

From our experience, even if you are a great listener, there is a good chance the rest of your team isn't. Building your "listening muscle" takes time and dedication. There are three disciplines to the practice of deep listening:

1. Listen to understand.
2. Be vulnerable with each other.
3. Stop having Either/Or arguments.

The first, listening to understand, lays the groundwork for the other two.

1. Listen to Understand

Almost everyone we work with is surprised to discover they haven't been listening as well as they think. This is backed up by research. A study of eight thousand employees found that most participants believed they were "above average" at listening, but their listening efficiency was only 25 percent.[20]

We observe that low-performing teams do not listen to each other. Usually, we see everyone looking at the person who is speaking. They might even hear what that person is saying, but they are not *listening*. This is what Stephen Covey, author of *The 7 Habits of Highly Effective People*, meant when he said, "Most people do not listen with the intent to understand; they listen with the intent to reply." Many people who believe they are listening are more accurately "sitting quietly waiting to speak." Or, they've checked out, thinking about all the other stuff they need to do. Maybe you catch yourself doing this sometimes?

In 2003, psychologist Faye Doell distinguished between the two types of listening Covey is referring to: **listening to understand** and listening to respond. According to Doell, people who listen to understand form stronger relationships and are more empathetic. The higher-performing teams we work with prioritize this kind of empathetic listening. The stronger the understanding and empathy on the team, the greater the trust. And the stronger the empathy, the better the engagement: 81 percent of employees reported being more willing to work long hours if they felt their employer was empathetic.[21]

Deep listening requires that you listen with the intention of understanding. Instead of formulating your opinion while someone is talking, focus on understanding *why* someone is saying what they're saying. In the next practice, we'll unpack the concept of the Fundamental Why—which is *why we do what we do*. By tuning in to a person's Fundamental Why, you can empathize with that person's point of view. This means listening for the answer to the question:

☐ Why is what they are saying important to them?

Remember earlier when we said these practices are not hard, but sometimes require a different way of thinking about things? This is an example of that. Instead of jumping in with your opinion or retort, listening to understand requires that you listen differently. To successfully execute this practice, listen with the goal of repeating back what you heard in a way that shows the speaker you understood.

Here is a very straightforward method to ensure you are listening to understand:

1. **Focus**: While the person is speaking, keep your attention focused on what the person is saying, not the thoughts in your head. *We highly recommend you get in the habit of taking notes while people are talking.*

2. **Repeat**: "You are saying [repeat back what they said]."

3. **Say out loud the Fundamental Why you heard**: "It sounds like this is important to you because..."

(Hang tight—you'll read all about this in the next practice.)

4. **Clarify**: "Did I get that right?" (They probably have more to add.)

The fourth step is essential. In most cases, you won't hear everything correctly. By clarifying what you heard, you give the person an opportunity to correct any miscommunication.

Listening to understand builds trust and communication in every conversation: when a request is being made, in a sales call, in team meetings, and in any situation where you want to be confident that communication has taken place.

Imagine if everyone on your team listened to understand whenever a client or someone from another department made a request. Imagine if everyone on your team listened to understand when making requests of each other. How quickly do you think communication would improve? How much extra, wasted work could be eliminated due to the *actual* communication that takes place when your team uses this one simple practice? Can you see how there would be less conflict and more collaboration? Can you imagine how trust would develop, and a culture of open honesty would become the norm, far more than you think is possible right now?

One time, a CEO called us in because she was dealing with a high level of conflict between a member of her executive team and a senior director from a different department. For months, both the executive and the senior director had been coming to her individually with complaints about the other. The conflicts between the two had escalated to the point where meetings that included them were overheated and unproductive. While the two were friendly in social situations, it seemed like there was no way they could work together.

When we first sat down with the three of them, we heard two different sides of the story.

The senior director said, pointing to the executive, "My team has been working for weeks on this redesign, and suddenly we get word he wants to cancel the whole project. This is completely unprofessional, and we are not going to shut down just because he wants us to."

"That's beside the point," the executive retorted. "The whole thing was off the mark. You're not considering that the clients I'm working with don't want this. You seem to be out of touch with what we need."

The first part of the conversation went back and forth like this. Each person sat waiting for the other to finish talking so they could jump in with a loud, confrontational response. Each launched into lengthy rants about everything the other person was doing wrong.

Finally, we asked both to stop talking, and we changed the rules of the game. "For the next forty-five minutes, you do not get to respond with your own point of view until you have successfully repeated back the Fundamental Why of what the other person is saying."

At first, they were annoyed with us and were reluctant to stick to the new rule. They each had a lot to say and wanted to respond right away with their own opinions. When they did, we cut them off, reminding them of the deep listening experiment we were conducting. Slowly, the vibe in the room got calmer as they got the hang of it.

"It sounds like you're frustrated," the senior director said to the executive. "You want to provide a great product to customers outside the US, and you don't think my team understands the broader market. Did I get that right?"

When it was the executive's turn, he said, "It sounds like what's important to you about this situation is that your team has been working on this for months. You think the work is good, and you believe I am just shutting it down because I am taking it personally. But fundamentally, you want what I want: to provide the best possible product to all our customers both inside and outside the US."

This conversation wasn't easy. Both of them needed to be humble enough to hear different points of view. When they finally got what the other was saying, both could see they shared a commitment to the same thing: a product that impresses their customers, both domestic and international. While they saw different ways to get there, they agreed they wanted the same results. From there, they could consider together: "How do we achieve what we both want?"

Their work together over the next few months changed completely. They stopped working in a vacuum and prioritized making their shared Fundamental Why the focus of every conversation. And they had *a lot more* conversations now that they understood they were working toward a shared goal. If the executive felt something about the product wouldn't connect with customers, he shared his concern with the senior director, knowing he would want to hear that feedback before his team spent too much time on a feature that wouldn't work. And with a clear understanding of *why* they needed to pivot, the senior director was happy to redirect his team if it meant it would get them closer to a successful product. Though it took a few months of collaborative effort—and really listening to each other—they found a solution that worked for both departments.

Listening to understand is the foundation for building trust and open communication. It's the key to turning arguments into productive conversations, no matter how many sides there are. Any time we've been called in to mediate high-heat executive conflicts, we don't move on from one person until they have clearly exhibited this kind of deep listening. While this might seem frustrating at first, the results usually lead to more innovative solutions than either party could have found on their own. This kind of listening is at the heart of great collaboration.

Deep listening involves the heart *and* the mind; it's both empathetic and logical. It's active, not passive. You engage with presence, openness, and attentiveness. You repeat back what you heard and what you think they meant. When you practice deep listening, the speaker feels heard, understood, and respected.

When your team practices this one skill, the team environment becomes psychologically safe.

Over time, a team intuition emerges; when everyone truly listens to each other, they make decisions that are more inclusive than competitive—and more spot on. The teams that get *really* good at deep listening sometimes tell us they can practically "read each other's minds."

Listening to understand takes tremendous discipline. It's not hard to do, but you have to catch yourself when you get distracted by your own thoughts and opinions. It also requires the humility to put your own perspective aside to hear—and understand—what's important to someone else.

2. Be Vulnerable

The highest-performing teams we work with are those most willing to be vulnerable with each other. This has been validated by the research Daniel Coyle presents in his book *The Culture Code*. After studying some of the world's most successful groups, including corporations, sports teams, and even the Navy SEALs, he concluded that "exchanges vulnerability, which we naturally tend to avoid, are the pathway through which trusting cooperation is built."[22]

Teams that cooperate better together are higher performing, which is why the second key discipline for this practice is to *be vulnerable*.

Sometimes people shudder when we use the word "vulnerability." But your team's ability to Get Real with Each Other depends on everyone's ability to be vulnerable enough to say what needs to be said. When everyone is willing to take risks and open up, it builds the psychological safety required to have conversations where people listen to, understand, and respect each other. It's what enables you to Get Real with Each Other.

We once worked with an executive team made up of five men and one woman, a team that enjoyed each other's company inside and outside of work. But we noticed something was off in a meeting when Shonna seemed unusually quiet. Halfway through the meeting, she shared an idea the team dismissed with an off-handed joke.

We paused the meeting and asked her, "Is there something you aren't saying but wish you could?"

When we asked her this, the room grew silent. She looked down at her notebook, took a deep breath, looked up, and said, "I don't know if it's okay to say this, but I've been holding back saying it for a long time. You know I enjoy working with you, but sometimes it feels like a boys' club here. The things you talk about don't always seem professional. Sometimes, I wonder if my being a woman is an impediment. It seems like I have to talk louder than all of you, or I won't get heard. Once you guys get going, it feels like I'm not even in the room. And Paul, the jokes you make are kind of offensive, but I don't want to be the one who brings everyone down. I just had to finally say this."

As she spoke, a couple of the executives were nodding their heads in a show of agreement. They immediately knew what she was talking about.

Paul had a look of shock on his face.

On lower-performing teams, this kind of feedback often makes people feel defensive. They take it as an attack. Paul and the others might have aggressively tried to convince her she was wrong. By this point, though, we had spent significant time practicing deep listening and building trust.

Still, the silence in the room was deafening.

Finally, with tears in his eyes, Paul said, "I am so sorry, Shonna. I honestly had no idea how you felt. I really enjoy working with you, and I would never want you to feel uncomfortable. I can absolutely change."

The rest of the team agreed it could be different as well, and the CEO publicly thanked her for her courage at that moment. In this specific instance, they truly hadn't known how she felt. Going forward, informed by what had previously been unsaid, things were different. The men's behavior in meetings changed, and the female executive found the environment far more welcoming. She told us afterward it was one of the most vulnerable moments of her career; a weight she had been carrying for two years suddenly lifted. It surprised her that all it took was one conversation.

BE A BETTER TEAM BY FRIDAY

Had the team members immediately defended themselves, you can be sure she'd never have felt safe enough to speak up again. But this was a high-performing team that valued openness and vulnerability. Despite the difficult feedback, Paul practiced deep listening to understand Shonna. As a result, he heard what she said, and made it safe for her to be vulnerable. Sometimes, all it takes is one open, honest conversation sharing "unsaids" like this one to dissolve longstanding frustrations or resentments.

You might be thinking, sure, this all sounds good on paper, but how do we get our team to actually *do* it? How do we create a healthier environment of psychological safety?

Pat Lencioni, the author of *The Five Dysfunctions of a Team*, suggests building **vulnerability-based trust**, which "requires team members to make themselves vulnerable to one another and be confident that their respective vulnerabilities will not be used against them."[23] These vulnerabilities include weaknesses, shortcomings, and requests for help. Additionally, when a leader admits they're fallible and human, they let others know it's okay to be imperfect themselves. The more open team members are with each other, the more this vulnerability-based trust will increase.

Building vulnerability-based trust requires intentionally setting aside time to get to know each other at a deeper level. We recommend beginning this process by conducting some version of a "Lifeline" exercise. In this exercise, everyone listens while one person talks. One by one, each team member shares three high points of their lives and three low points. Tell the story of each. Share as much as you are willing to share. Challenge yourself to be vulnerable.

Here is how we lead the Lifeline exercise. The leader of the team always goes first. We challenge this leader to push the boundaries of what they're comfortable with sharing, since they set the tone for the rest of the group.

1. Every person draws a horizontal line across a sheet of paper. Label "0" on the left, "NOW" on the right. This represents your chronological life.

2. Consider three highs in your career or personal life that you're willing to share. Put a dot on the line in the appropriate spot in your lifeline and write a note indicating what that event is so you can talk about it.

3. Consider three obstacles or roadblocks in your career or personal life that you had to overcome to make you who you are today (*that you are willing to share*). This might have been a challenging time, but you made it through and learned from it. Put a dot on the line at the appropriate spot in your lifeline and write a note indicating what that event is so you can talk about it.

4. Ask that everyone agree to maintain confidentiality in these conversations. Make sure everyone says, "I agree."

5. Go around the circle and have one person at a time share the story of these life events while everyone

else listens. Each person shares two or three highs and two or three obstacles. Whoever is leading this exercise goes first! The authenticity and depth of your share gives everyone else permission to share authentically as well.

Every single time we've led this exercise, the feeling and tone in the group shift. People become quiet and focused; a solemnity and reverence emerge.

When teams complete the exercise, we hear things like:

"I feel closer with my team than I ever have."

"This will change how we work together forever."

"I've worked with this person for years, and I see him as a human being for the first time."

Certainly, teams that have worked together for a long time will benefit greatly. But we have found that some form of personal history exercise like the Lifeline builds trust quickly when there Isn't much time. For instance, when we work on cross-functional projects, people from different departments are thrown together and expected to produce results quickly. We believe it's a must for any brand-new team to do this exercise and continue to find time to practice exchanges of vulnerability.

After doing a Lifeline exercise with your team, continue to find opportunities for personal shares to build vulnerability-based trust. Set aside time to ask each other questions that require you to be vulnerable to answer. While these questions may sound formulaic on paper, the answers can open a rich opportunity for building deeper trust:

☐ "What has been your greatest accomplishment in your career, and what was so important about it to you?"

☐ "Why do you love the kind of work you do?"

☐ "What are you most passionate about in your life outside of work?"

☐ "When have you overcome a particular obstacle, and what strength did you exhibit to overcome it?"

As trust builds, consider asking more personal questions about their families, their personal lives, their hopes, and their dreams:

☐ "What do you love about your children?"

☐ "Who influenced you the most growing up, and why were they important to you?"

☐ "What is your favorite childhood memory?"

☐ "Who was your childhood hero and why?"

The more trust builds, the more personal these conversations can become.

We once worked with a fast-growing US engineering company. They were going through a merger and acquisition that united multiple companies into one, and they had become a top 15 firm in their industry nationwide. We were brought in from the get-go before any real team camaraderie had been formed. In the first meeting, multiple heads of companies were in the room, each with their own priorities. They did not know each other well and had only worked together on occasion, if at all. Despite this, they had to come together as a team to quickly figure out how to make a national impact.

One of the first things we did with this group was to lead the Lifeline exercise. When we asked each team member to openly share personal highs and lows in their life, a nervous tension descended upon the group. These company leaders were strangers, and we were asking them to tell each other personal stories about themselves.

The CEO had articulated a commitment that the company's culture would be one where people cared about each other. Over the course of about twenty minutes, he shared stories about his greatest prides and difficulties, personal stories about his family and his own life. As he talked, many in the room were moved to tears, and his example set the tone. Over the next two hours, a group of near strangers shared stories with each other about their own lives. Everyone felt the newly built trust among them. In one afternoon, what had been a slightly adversarial group came together as a team.

Two years later, the company went public. This CEO told us that this early, vulnerable conversation was critical to achieving such a far-reaching goal. That sometimes awkward, sometimes difficult personal storytelling laid the groundwork for relating to each other with the vulnerability necessary to have open conversations. Their willingness to engage in a vulnerability exchange as strangers helped them understand that their decisions needed to come from the heart, which became a core value of the company.

Consider the adage that trust takes time to build and only a second to break. For a team to create an environment of psychological safety and communication that leads to high performance, they must practice vulnerable exchanges in *every* conversation. Being vulnerable in a Lifeline exercise is important, but won't effect cultural change if differing, uncomfortable points of view get shut down in all other meetings.

3. Stop Having Either/Or Arguments

Lower-performing team meetings often dissolve into a series of arguments. Sometimes, voices slowly get louder and louder until the tension gets so thick the discussion becomes confrontational. The people arguing leave these meetings feeling more justified in their own point of view, and the quiet ones leave feeling marginalized. Rarely do conflicts get resolved.

At the heart of all this arguing is a simple equation called **Either/Or.** This approach keeps people locked into right and wrong, which blocks the ability to find common ground. It looks like this:

- *Either* I agree with you, *or* I disagree with you.
- *Either* you agree with me, *or* you disagree with me.
- *Either* I am right, *or* you are right.
- It is *either* your way *or* mine. Prove to me I'm wrong or agree with me.

On lower-performing teams, people try harder (and speak louder) to gain consensus on their own point of view. Often, those with the most dominant voices and best debating skills "win."

But if you think about it, your point of view is *always* your point of view. Someone else has a different point of view, and from their perspective, *they're* right. The way they think and feel about an issue simply makes more sense to them than how you think and feel about it.

Both of you have had unique experiences that led you to your personal conclusions, and you each have a Personal Fundamental Why behind what you are saying. In some way, you're *both* right, but you can't find the common ground to see that because of an Either/Or way of thinking.

The third discipline of deep listening cuts through these arguments, shifting from Either/Or to what we call **Both/And**.

High-performing teams are committed to including perspectives from all sides. We call this gathering a **collective point of view**. (This might also be called an "executive point of view.") Executives must be able to see the organization as a whole, not only from the perspective of their own function. The highest-performing executive teams don't waste time arguing over who is right. They consider as many perspectives as possible and make insightful, clear decisions based on what they've learned.

The collective point of view allows teams to operate as "greater than the sum of their parts." It's at the heart of collaboration. To take a collective point of view, teams must actively choose to switch from Either/Or listening to Both/And:

- *Both* your perspective *and* mine are valid, from our own points of view. What can we learn from each other?
- *Both* your underlying intention (Fundamental Why) *and* my underlying intention are necessary to consider. How can we include both? What do our different perspectives have in common?

To listen for this kind of Both/And understanding, you listen for the answer to the questions:

☐ *"Why is what he's saying important to him?"*
   (listening to understand)
☐ *"How might her perspective have some truth to it?"*
☐ *"What can I learn from their perspective?"*

This kind of listening isn't easy, especially when the stakes are high and team members have competing priorities. Competing priorities lead to entrenched perspectives that escalate into conflict—fast. Most teams *do* argue from time to time, but higher-performing teams get out of conflict and into resolution much more quickly because they've learned how to expand their points of view. They don't need to be right all the time because they understand that Both/And means they aren't wrong—or even necessarily right. Rather, each person's point of view is a piece of a larger puzzle, and by committing to Both/And, the team benefits from the intelligence of the entire team.

Gathering this kind of collective point of view requires a commitment to the practice of deep listening. The key indicator that you've fallen out of the practice is back-and-forth arguing. As soon as an argument begins, you must intentionally go back to the basic, foundational practice of deep listening.

We worked with a company where the CEO and the VP of Marketing had a particular point of view about the direction the company should take, and the rest of the leadership team saw things so differently that people quit. Morale was down, trust was low, and deadlines were missed.

At first, the CEO was adamant: the problem was that he was surrounded by people who didn't know anything about marketing. He spent meeting after meeting trying to convince everyone to see his and the VP's point of view. Every meeting turned into a heated spat; emotions ran high, and nobody was happy. When someone quit, the CEO saw it as proof he was right—they just didn't get it.

But in private, the rest of the leadership team told us a different story. They said the CEO had liked some of the VP of Marketing's ideas early on and grew overly excited about them. This early enthusiasm turned into a kind of "us vs. them" dynamic, pitting the two of them against the rest of the team. The CEO shaped his decisions almost wholly on the advice of the VP. Rather than take input from the whole team, he had started over-prioritizing the VP's opinion. He argued against any point of view that seemed contradictory. The leadership team had lost faith that the CEO could be objective in his point of view.

When we worked one-on-one with the CEO, we encouraged him to embrace Both/And listening. We challenged him to listen for a collective point of view. We asked him to practice deep listening to expand his perspective to include Both/And:

1. What is the point of view of each person on your team?
2. What is the Fundamental Why of that point of view?
3. How might their point of view have some truth in it?
4. What can you learn from it?

When the CEO began to embrace Both/And listening, he came to us with a realization. He saw what his team members had already shared: he was over-valuing one point of view. He told us he had not seen this, but the VP of Marketing spoke in a way that naturally divided people. That VP used Either/Or argumentation. At first, this gave the CEO more confidence in the VP's position, but now the CEO saw how the VP's dominant style overshadowed the less charismatic team members' opinions. He also had not noticed how much the VP's tendency to argue deflated the rest of the team.

The CEO had been unaware of this dynamic until he shifted from Either/Or to Both/And. From that point forward, the team developed a shared voice. The CEO took time to practice deep listening in meetings, making sure he understood the Fundamental Why of each person's perspective. When arguments erupted, he asked the team to pause and practice listening to understand each other.

Meanwhile, the VP of Marketing grew upset. He was not open to trying a new way of listening and ended up leaving the team when his argumentative style no longer fit with their Both/And culture. Afterward, the CEO admitted he'd allowed a toxic team member to denigrate his team. As a result, the team's meetings and collaboration dramatically improved.

Of course, decisions *must* be made. The course of action a team decides to take will often require Either/Or thinking. But the choice to move in a particular direction means that you are also choosing what not to do. Both/And leads to better decision-making: when you see multiple points of view, you make choices that consider the pros and cons of various options. On a team with competing priorities like the one in this story, Both/And allowed the CEO to see a larger, more collective point of view so that his decisions could better reflect the opinions of everyone on the team, not just one individual.

Listening to understand, being vulnerable, and shifting from Either/Or arguments to Both/And thinking require a commitment from everyone. Without these, your team members will likely experience the environment on your team as psychologically unsafe. On the other hand, with consistent practice, the collaboration, productivity, and happiness factor on your team will surpass anything you have seen yet.

PRACTICE TWO

GET REAL WITH EACH OTHER

STRUCTURE FOR APPLICATION

1. Work on building trust among your team by treating leadership like a conversation.

2. As a team, learn and practice some form of deep listening together.

3. Conduct a Lifeline exercise or other personal history exercise.

4. During meetings, prioritize gaining a collective point of view by listening for understanding Both/And versus listening for agreement or disagreement Either/Or.

5. Any time arguing ensues, immediately revert to your deep listening practice. Make sure everyone understands the Fundamental Why of each person's perspective.

6. As long as you are a team, continue regularly practicing vulnerability exchanges through personal history shares. Remember that "we did that six months ago" means you are not doing it as a practice. Choose new questions to answer as a team that support a deepening of trust.

THREE

KNOW THE "FUNDAMENTAL WHY"

"When I was younger there was something in me. I had passion. I may not have known what I was going to do with that passion, but there was something—and I still feel it. It's this little engine that roars inside of me, and I just want to keep going and going."
—SHEILA JOHNSON, president of the Washington Mystics and co-founder of BET

Disengaged employees take a toll on your company and your teams. As you stroll through your office, do you often find a lackluster, slightly grumpy vibe in the air? Do people show up to video meetings looking like they're already ready to leave? If so, you've probably tried everything you could think of to increase engagement: give bonuses, buy a foosball table, install beer on tap, offer flexible work hours, try pep talks, push harder, add more rules and processes. Still, you get the sense that the people working for you are not entirely excited about what they're doing.

Sure, people are working, but *something* is missing.

According to Galup's 142-country State of the Global Workforce study, only 13 percent of workers globally are fully engaged at work. Sixty-three percent of employees across the globe are disengaged, and 24 percent of these are actively disengaged at work. ("Actively disengaged" means that they actively undermine their engaged colleagues and spread negativity to others.)[24] In our work with CEOs, senior executives, directors, and managers, one of the most common questions we hear is, "How do I motivate my team?"

Motivation is an inside job. When someone is self-motivated, they're driven by an internal engine. They aren't doing something because they're *supposed* to; they do it because they *want* to.

So how *do* you motivate your team?

The key to motivating others is learning how to connect with their inner drive. In his book *The Fifth Discipline*, Peter Senge refers to this internal drive when he talks about "tapping into" people's deepest commitment and ability to learn.[25] This is **intrinsic motivation**, driven by something inside rather than an external incentive like money or fame.

When you're *externally* motivated, you act with the hopes of receiving a reward or avoiding punishment. When you're *intrinsically* motivated, you act because you want to. Both have value. Offering bonuses and performance incentives does motivate a team.

However, when you offer rewards and still feel something is missing, you need to discover what intrinsically motivates the people you work with. When people start complaining about your incentives and stop trying to earn them, you know you've got a problem. (Bonuses are too small! The bar is too high! The perks aren't as good as company XYZ!)

So how do you inspire a culture of intrinsic motivation among your team members, in your company, and perhaps most importantly, within yourself? Know the Fundamental Why.

Prioritizing the Fundamental Why is critical for employee engagement and retention—two significant struggles for fast-growing companies. If you're a CEO or top executive, it makes sense that one of your top motivators would be company growth. Your employees, however, need much more than company metrics to keep them engaged with their work (and really, so do you).

Top leaders have highly motivated teams because they keep this one question at the center of their work:

What is the Fundamental Why?

They listen for the answer to this when communicating with others. They prioritize communicating *their* Why at all times, understand *everyone else's* Why, and align *their team* around the Why behind everything they do.

When this happens, teams become excited about their work again. Each member feels seen and heard. They are eager to own the team's success and help their peers succeed, too. That grumpy vibe dissipates. Teams become united around a shared purpose, and team members feel their work has personal meaning. Yes, one question can achieve all of this. You just need to take the time to ask about, listen for, and share the Fundamental Why.

WHY WE DO WHAT WE DO

We use the term Fundamental Why to simply mean "the underlying purpose or intention."

Every person has a Fundamental Why they do what they do. Every request has a Fundamental Why. Every meeting and project *should* have a Fundamental Why, or you should delete it from the docket (more on this in Practice 6: Getting Focused). Every team has a Fundamental Why, or it wouldn't exist.

Organizations have Fundamental Whys, too. An organization's Fundamental Why is usually its purpose or mission statement. Disney's purpose is, "We create happiness." SpaceX has a Fundamental Why that would truly change life as we know it: to "revolutionize space technology with the ultimate goal of enabling people to live on other planets."

A company's Fundamental Why creates a shared understanding across the organization, a core intention for employees to return to when they temporarily lose their sense of purpose.

Like great organizations, teams and projects should have well-articulated Fundamental Whys, too. The Fundamental Why gets to the root of why you're doing what you're doing. A team's Fundamental Why is what unites and aligns the team; it's usually a common, aspirational goal. Pat Lencioni, author of *The Five Dysfunctions of a Team*, says, "If you could get all the people in the organization rowing in the same direction, you could dominate any industry, in any market, against any competition, at any time."[26] The team's Fundamental Why is the backbone of this alignment.

As you zoom in from the broad, organizational level down to the individuals that make the company, every layer has a Fundamental Why.

A meeting has a Fundamental Why (e.g., to move us into phase two of the development project by aligning around next step actions).

A project has a Fundamental Why (e.g., to improve organizational effectiveness by moving all business processes into one central software platform).

Even every single request you make has a Fundamental Why that answers the question:

"Why is this request important to the person making it?"

Unfortunately, requests are often made without including the Fundamental Why—and it's a huge oversight. Think about the last time you asked somebody to do something for you. Did you articulate *why* you were asking? How about the last time someone made a request of you? Was there a Fundamental Why included? Our experience shows that if you were unclear about your Fundamental Why, the person on the other end of that request was, too.

When the purpose of a request is clear, you're asking for someone's support in helping you fulfill something bigger than a mere task. When you share your Fundamental Why, people understand why your request is so important to you and are more inclined to take ownership of the job and ensure it's done well. If you ask your colleague to make some copies for you to impress a huge client prospect, your colleague needs to know the underlying purpose of that request. Your colleague will probably pay more attention to detail than if the copies were for an internal meeting.

Adding a few words to clarify the *Why* of your requests is a tiny change that can have a giant impact on your day-to-day efficiency. It alleviates confusion. It cuts time spent on things that don't matter. It keeps everyone's focus aligned around a shared goal.

We worked with a team that brought in an outside graphic designer to build their website. At first, the team had very clear requests: five different tabs, a clear color palette, and a clean and professional treatment of the content. The designer gave them precisely what they asked for, and, on the surface, the work was strong. But the team had the sense that it wasn't quite right, and the back and forth between them became nitpicky and terse. No one was happy, and the team had gotten to the point where they wondered if they should start over with a new designer.

"From the looks of it," we said, "your designer did exactly what you asked. What's the problem?"

They couldn't identify it.

We probed further. "It looks like your designer is very clear on what you are asking for, but how clear is she on *why* you need it in the first place?"

The team admitted they had made a lot of requests without including the conversation about the Fundamental Why. So they took a step back and invited the designer in to talk about the underlying intention for the project.

The team explained to the designer that they didn't just want the site to be a calling card. They wanted it to show how their product was different and how they had a new way of thinking. Almost immediately, the designer began enthusiastically drawing a new site map on the board. The team loved it, and the finished website was a company showcase far exceeding what they had originally imagined.

Afterward, the designer admitted, "I have ten different clients. This website was just another task on my to-do list, and I was frustrated by the team's tedious feedback. After that meeting, though, I got excited. There was an opportunity for me to contribute my creativity and expertise that hadn't been there before. It went from feeling like I was slogging my way through a task to feeling like I could hit a home run."

In this case, knowing the Fundamental Why led to a level of intrinsic motivation that wasn't there before. At first, the designer was externally motivated to get the job done and satisfy the client. After learning the team's Fundamental Why, her motivation shifted from external to intrinsic.

DO YOU KNOW THE FUNDAMENTAL WHY OF EACH INDIVIDUAL YOU WORK WITH?

All individuals have a **Personal Fundamental Why**. Often, saying it out loud for the first time can be surprisingly energizing. Most people have never actually spoken it out loud. When you do, though, it just sounds right. Sometimes, the managers we coach are moved to tears when they find words to describe their Fundamental Why. They say things like, "That's it! That's why I have always done what I do!"

Simon Sinek, author of *Start with Why*, said, "There are only two ways to influence human behavior: you can manipulate it, or you can inspire it."[27] You can't force someone to be inspired. However, you can discover what inspires them, and help them experience more of this. To learn what motivates someone requires you to ask—and listen.

Here are some questions to get you started:

1. "What do you love about your job? Why?"
2. "When do you get so immersed in a project you lose track of time?"

3. "What do you love about that kind of work?"
4. "What did you love to do as a kid, and how does that relate to the work you do now?"
5. "What have been some challenges in your life, and what strengths did you use to overcome them?"

Many people see a connection between some of their favorite childhood activities or school subjects and their current work. We've talked with chief financial officers who loved math more than any other kid in the class, engineers who played with erector sets and LEGOS, creative directors who loved to paint, and human resources managers who loved taking care of friends. One entrepreneurial CEO we worked with told us she started her first company at age six, and that her parents were her only clients.

The CFO who loved math said his Fundamental Why was "to make numbers work for people."

An engineer wanted "to solve the most difficult problems I can."

A creative director was all about "making things more beautiful."

An HR manager said, "so people live their best lives at work."

The CEO who started a business at age six said her Fundamental Why was "to do something that's never been done before."

Sometimes it's even closer to the heart:

"Everything I do is for my family."

"To be of service."

"To make the world a better place for future generations."

Whatever motivated you early in life likely still motivates you now in some way. While our interests and jobs might change many times throughout our lives, the spark that drives us to learn and improve often traces back to childhood. That spark helps us all choose the careers we're in—if we're lucky. If you're not sure what your Personal Fundamental Why is, ask yourself the question:

☐ "Why do I do what I do?"

It's okay if an answer doesn't immediately come to mind. The question can feel intimidating if you've never stopped to reflect on your work in this way. Here are some other questions to consider as you make your way to your Fundamental Why:

> ☐ "Besides a paycheck, what is important to me about the work I do?"
> ☐ "What achievements do I feel most proud of?"
> ☐ "What professional obstacle have I overcome that's made me who I am today? Why was that such an important moment in my career?"

When we explore these fundamental drives in our workshops, we ask managers: "Why would it be of value to learn the **Fundamental Why** of each person you work with?"

Common reasons we hear include:

- "You would know what motivates them."
- "You could find ways for them to do more of what they love."
- "You could build deeper trust and collaborate better."
- "You could show them you care about them."

These are all true; most people we work with intuitively know this. When someone's Personal Fundamental Why aligns with their work, they come alive. It makes them happier, more engaged, and more focused.

Then we ask those managers:

"Do you confidently Know the Fundamental Why of each person you work with?"

At that question, we see maybe one or two heads nod in a group of fifty. For the most part, managers, directors, and executives have no idea what intrinsically motivates the people who work with them. Most of them agree that because they aren't clear on intrinsic motivators, they mistakenly resort to trying to motivate their employees with more demands and rules. Or they try to be overly nice and hope that will help.

Whole Foods Market CEO John Mackey said, "If you are lucky enough to be someone's employer, then you have a moral obligation to make sure people look forward to coming to work in the morning."[28] Getting to know each team member's Fundamental Why is the way to start. When you understand what fundamentally inspires someone, you can work to assign tasks, projects, and roles that naturally engage them. The more they do what they love, the more they look forward to coming to work.

One senior director we worked with, Leo, had a reputation of being difficult to work for. We knew his intentions were good, but he would complain that if he didn't push his team hard, they wouldn't do the work. He also admitted he didn't know the Personal Fundamental Why of the individuals on his team.

So, we suggested he find out. He held one-on-one conversations with every one of his nineteen direct reports. When he came back to us with his insights, he couldn't believe how little he really knew about the people who worked for him. Once he got everyone's

Fundamental Why, he saw that many of them were doing the wrong work. So, he started assigning work in a way that he now sees best aligns with what motivates each of them.

Leo was surprised to learn that his CPA, Elena, got into doing what she did because her Fundamental Why was to "solve really complicated problems" for her clients. As the company scaled, he needed someone to put on large, complex accounts where clients were feeling frustrated.

After learning Elena's Why, Leo assigned her to work with a client struggling to implement the new software they purchased from Leo's company.

Leo said Elena's eyes lit up when he asked if she would be interested in taking on that challenge. Up until that point, Elena had been assigned to do accounting and financial analyst work that didn't present her with any challenges to solve. She was clearly bored. Recently, she spoke at a meeting for the first time in months to share a milestone. She had turned a frustrated client into a referenceable client in sixty days.

As Leo worked on understanding each employee's Fundamental Why, he moved another team member, Celia, off of a project centered on analyzing a client's cash flow. Celia had shared that she got into the finance business because she loved making numbers make sense through teaching. Now Celia is helping a different client write a training program for their new hires.

Leo shared that after only one month, he noticed a lot more participation in meetings. A couple of people even stopped by his office just to say hi.

Another leader we work with, Jordan, uses the Fundamental Why to help with employee retention. She's made it a part of her interview process to ask people their Fundamental Why, and to share her own with them. She finds that it's a quick, powerful way to establish trust and get to know each other beyond the surface. She also feels that it communicates to interviewees that her team fosters a company culture that puts people first.

Jordan shared with us that since she's incorporated the Fundamental Why into her interviews, she's been able to assign tasks to each employee that align with their *Why* from the start, keeping them motivated and engaged in their work from day one.

You won't always be able to assign work to each team member that fits their Why. And you don't always have to. Simply knowing their Why and keeping it a priority will make a difference. If someone's Why revolves around his family, ask him about his family. What is he most proud of? What would he want his kids to know about the kind of work he does? Find ways to tie in what matters most to someone, and you'll find what motivates them. Help them connect the dots to see that what they're doing on your team matters, and that there are ways to bring more of what's important to them into the game.

There is always a way to connect with someone's Why. The big mistake many leaders make is never finding out their team members' Why. Take the time to ask each person. Also, tell them your Why. These are the conversations that build trust and pull teams out of being average.

ESTABLISH YOUR TEAM'S FUNDAMENTAL WHY

Without a doubt, the highest-performing teams are made up of individuals whose Personal Fundamental Why most closely aligns with the team's Fundamental Why. When individuals believe *their* purpose supports the team's purpose, intrinsic motivation goes way up.

Usually, when we first start working with lower-performing teams, the team's Fundamental Why is lackluster and uninspiring, or team members have lost touch with it entirely.

Sometimes, the team had no Fundamental Why to begin with. We've led many trainings on the Fundamental Why, and when we ask, "What is your team's Fundamental Why?" participants look at us with bewildered faces. They say things like, "I have no clue. We're just doing what we're doing because it's our job."

When this is the case, people feel adrift in their roles. They're busy, stressed, and full of to-dos, but they can't always remember *why* they're doing so much in the first place. They lack a sense of purpose in their work. Boredom, mediocre performance, and indifference set in, ultimately infecting the entire company and causing people to quit.

High-performing teams, on the other hand, have clearly articulated the team's Fundamental Why. Perhaps more importantly, when each member's Personal Fundamental Why aligns with the team's, it serves as a tuning fork, energizing and motivating everybody. We all want to do work that matters to us, to the team, and to the company.

In *The Fifth Discipline*, Peter Senge puts it this way, "When you ask people about what it is like being part of a great team, what is most striking is the meaningfulness of the experience. People talk about being part of something larger than themselves, of being connected, of being generative. It becomes quite clear that, for many, their experiences as part of truly great teams stand out as singular periods of life lived to the fullest."[29]

People want to know the work they do serves an underlying purpose. As Daniel Pink points out in his book *Drive*, "We leave lucrative jobs to take low-paying ones that provide a clearer sense of purpose."[30]

To become high performing, a team must first do the work of identifying the team's Fundamental Why. Ask yourselves as a team;

"Why are we doing what we're doing?"

Examples of great team Fundamental Whys we have heard:

- "To bring the world's best customer service to our clients."
- "To make sure every interaction with our software is seamless."
- "To have every person at the company love their job."

This series of questions is particularly important for the executive team to reflect upon. Usually, the executive team's Fundamental Why defines the Fundamental Why of the organization. Sometimes, after workshopping their Fundamental Why, we have seen executive teams change the company's mission statement.

Examples of what some of our clients' Fundamental Whys look like:

- "To revolutionize the way people experience food." (Bypass Mobile)
- "To have a world where people can do what they love and achieve their dreams." (Tailos)
- "Payments professionals love." (AffiniPay)

No matter what business you are in or team you are on, the Fundamental Why should inspire. Ask:

- ☐ "How does the service or product we provide improve something?"
- ☐ "How will the work we do on this project improve our organization?"
- ☐ "How will this work improve our clients' or customers' businesses? Their lives?"
- ☐ "Why should we do this work in the first place?"

Start there.

Unforeseen obstacles arise at work all the time. External circumstances force you to adapt. A high-performance team's Fundamental Why is their North Star, a guide through the turbulence of change. Their dedication to an agreed-upon purpose unites them as a team. Where a lower-performing team falters when things get tough, the high-performance team stays true to their commitment.

COMMIT TO YOUR FUNDAMENTAL WHY

When your Personal Fundamental Why aligns with the team's, you experience increased energy, motivation, and a determination to make something happen. Without this alignment, it's difficult to gain true commitment. Commitment requires something greater than just *having* a sense of purpose. A commitment requires a willingness to take a stand and say, "I will do what it takes to bring this Fundamental Why to life." As Hall of Fame basketball coach Pat Riley said, "There are only two options regarding commitment; you're either in or you're out. There's no such thing as life in-between."

This type of buy-in holds the team together. When individuals on a team are personally committed to the team's purpose, the team excels in ways not possible before. This is true whether you're on a project team, department team, executive team, or cross-functional team. Without a clear, compelling Fundamental Why, there will be a lack of commitment—it won't be clear what you're committing to.

On high-performing teams, everyone is fully committed. On lower-performing teams, commitment wanes. Team members are less enthusiastic—and occasionally bitter. Until you do the work outlined in this practice, this friction will continue. If you work on a team that lacks commitment and enthusiasm, the first step is to ensure you know each person's Fundamental Why. Then work together to clarify the team's (or project's) Why. Ask each member of the team:

"What do you think is the Fundamental Why of this team [or project]?"

We often find that everyone on the *same* team has a *different* answer. When this happens, write out people's responses on a whiteboard or flipchart.

Next, share the various answers with your team and answer these questions as a group:

☐ "What commonalities do we see?"
☐ "What are the differences?"
☐ "What would be a clear, compelling Fundamental Why that everyone could agree to?"

We first experienced the full power of this practice early in our pre-BLUECASE careers consulting in global oil and gas companies. Many of the client teams we worked with were managing billion-dollar major capital projects, e.g., building a new wing at an international airport or building an offshore oil platform. These projects required teams to work with people across different companies, quite often from different countries. Unfortunately, projects like these often lead to workers getting injured. But our clients wanted it to be different.

Our work brought the leaders of these projects together to articulate *specifically* what they were committed to making happen. Of course, this commitment included a vision of project excellence with the work completed under budget and on time. But it also included a commitment to completing each project without harm to the workers. The projects often required a million plus hours of people's time to complete and were executed in extremely dangerous environments. But the leaders across the project stood by the same commitment: no one gets hurt. Because they shared this commitment, they made decisions that prioritized safety above all else. How they worked was shaped by their commitment. As a result of that commitment and hard work, the projects were, in fact, completed without injury. (If you want to learn more about this kind of life-saving safety work, visit *jmj.com*.)

A bold commitment can influence an entire culture. One of our clients has created a platform that relays detailed data almost instantaneously across emergency medical services, enabling patient data to arrive at the hospital before the ambulance pulls in. Their commitment is saving lives through this high-speed data delivery, and growing their company large enough that the global healthcare system benefits from the power of their data platform.

This firm is one of the fastest-growing companies of its size we have seen. Their work is demanding and, at times, high stress. Still, employee surveys showed that their culture has gotten stronger as they have grown from a local startup with thirty employees to a multinational company with over four hundred employees. We find working with this client invigorating because their employees know that what they do every day goes toward something larger than themselves. The engineers and developers of the platform appreciate that their work saves lives. The marketing team knows their creative ideas support the company's ability to save even more lives. The people resources department ensures that the right culture and processes are in place so they, too, can help save lives.

Your commitment does not need to be about saving lives to inspire a team. One of our clients, a professional payments platform company, is committed to unrivaled customer experience in everything they do. Your team could commit to customer service wait times that are less than one minute, or to making everything you produce more beautiful. You could even commit to running the best office anyone has ever experienced, which may or may not be directly related to your product or service. The key is to commit to something that inspires you and your team, and be unwavering in your pursuit. Be creative and bold, and clearly connect your commitment to the Fundamental Why of your company, your team, and yourself.

As a team ask:

☐ "What are we committed to as a team?"
☐ "What is our vision of what this will look like?"

☐ "How will our work better the lives of our customers and our coworkers?"

☐ "Why *must* it happen?"

Finally, ask yourself and each other:

☐ "What will it take for us each to commit to this fully?"

Stick with it until everyone agrees to a team commitment they can get behind. If you try to break one matchstick by itself, it snaps quickly. If you try to break a hundred matchsticks in one bundle, you can't. A shared commitment has this kind of strength.

One final note: a huge component of this practice is to revisit your Fundamental Why and "re-up" your commitment. Plan to do this regularly, particularly when you notice things have gotten hard and people are nearing burnout. During high-stress times, people are more likely to go home at night and vent. They start asking themselves, "Why am I putting up with this?" For this reason, never stop reminding yourselves of your commitment and the Fundamental Why behind it.

KNOW THE FUNDAMENTAL WHY

STRUCTURE FOR APPLICATION

1. Make sure every request you make of others has a clearly articulated Fundamental Why.

2. Take time to get to know each of your team members' Fundamental Why.

3. Give everyone the opportunity to share their Personal Fundamental Why with their team members, including managers.

4. As a team, create a clear articulation of your team's Fundamental Why.

5. Speak the commitment to your Fundamental Why out loud regularly and often. Share it with those outside your teams. Ask for their help in making your commitment happen.

6. Regularly revisit your commitment when things get tough. Have the right conversations to make sure that everyone has reconnected with this commitment.

7. BONUS: if you are in sales, business development, or customer success, discover the Fundamental Why of your customer or prospect.

GIVE FEEDBACK LIKE A COACH

"Average players want to be left alone. Good players want to be coached. Great players want to be told the truth."

—DOC RIVERS, coach of the Philadelphia 76ers

What would be possible if you had an almost magical ability to radically accelerate the performance of everyone on your team? What could you accomplish if the people who worked with you could greatly outperform other teams, have extremely high engagement, and make steep changes in their abilities almost overnight? What if you could at least double the speed at which you and those around you learn and develop?

That is the promise of this chapter. But getting these kinds of results often requires changing how you think of feedback. In fact, most common assumptions about how to improve performance are likely holding you back.

Imagine if someone walked into your office today and said, "I have some feedback for you." If you're like most people, hearing the word "feedback" fills you with dread. It makes you brace yourself, preparing for a heavy blow.

Right?

Everyone knows giving and receiving feedback is essential, but most people hate it because they're used to experiencing feedback as bad news. They associate feedback with phrases that start with, "What's wrong with this is...," or, "The problem is..." For most people, hearing opening lines like these are little shocks to the system. A study presented by *Harvard Business Review* shows that negative feedback activates the sympathetic nervous system, or "fight, flight, or freeze."[31] When people give us negative feedback, our bodies tell us to get defensive, get out of there, or completely shut down.

Simply put, the way most people give feedback makes the person hearing it feel bad. The activated fight, flight, or freeze mode impairs learning because, according to Case Western Reserve University organizational behavior and psychology professor Richard Boyatzis, the sympathetic nervous system "inhibits access to existing neural circuits and invokes cognitive, emotional, and perceptual impairment."[32]

So not only does negative feedback feel bad, *it probably won't work like you want it to* because people are less able to learn and absorb information in that reactive state.

Most of what we've learned about giving feedback reinforces low engagement, attrition, and mediocrity—exactly what leaders try to avoid in today's ever-changing work environments. You don't need to be stuck there, though. You can break the cycle the moment you choose to change your perspective on feedback.

Let's look at the dictionary definition of the word "feedback":

Feedback = information about reactions to a product, a person's performance of a task, etc., which is used as a basis for improvement.[33]

As you can see, the definition of feedback does not use the word "criticism." "Feedback" is a neutral term. Based on this definition, *feedback is information that leads to improvement.* If, as the study suggests, the type of feedback most people offer doesn't work to improve someone's performance, we need to find another way to give it.

Professional athletes receive far more performance feedback from their coaches and teammates on a day-to-day basis than most people do. Great athletes work with the best coaches because great coaches provide the best feedback—that is, feedback that *leads to improvement.*

The same can be said for company leaders: organizational leadership expert Ken Blanchard famously quotes his former consulting partner, Rick Tate, who said, "Feedback is the breakfast of champions."[34] Company leaders who want to excel at the highest levels prioritize gathering and applying feedback like a champion athlete. Knowing this, teams and individuals should be seeking out feedback every single day. Any information that leads to improvement is gold, isn't it?

But most of what gets called "feedback" doesn't work like this. Gallup found that only 26 percent of employees strongly agree that the feedback they receive helps them do better work.[35]

Why are employees not getting enough meaningful feedback? One reason is that feedback has become associated with quarterly or annual performance reviews tied to financial incentives.

Picture this: An employee has a two-hour block with her manager scheduled on the calendar for weeks in advance. She knows it's there but doesn't want to think about it. The day comes, and she walks into her manager's office with a smile on her face and a knot in her stomach. The meeting starts with friendly conversation. Then she sits quietly while her manager shares what's wrong with her performance. She gets a little defensive, but both parties slog through. Finally, she learns whether she is on track to get a raise or this year's bonus. Phew, that's over. She doesn't need to do that again for another year.

If you're only giving or receiving feedback at these quarterly or annual reviews like this, it's not enough—and may be hurting performance. According to Gallup's Robert Sutton and Ben Wigert, PhD, "Traditional performance reviews and approaches to feedback are often so bad that they *actually make performance worse about one-third of the time*" because of the lack of frequency and lack of skillful feedback.[36] Another Gallup study reveals that only 14 percent of employees strongly agree their performance reviews inspire them to improve.[37]

Clearly, the way feedback has been done historically doesn't work out as planned. But plenty of well-intentioned leaders also aren't giving enough feedback for a much more obvious reason: they don't want to make people feel bad or deal with the fallout of an emotional reaction. A manager may know there's an issue with one of her team members, since she has received numerous complaints about him. At first, she hopes the problem will fix itself, but over time it becomes clear it won't. Finally, the day comes when she has to say something to the employee. When she does, the employee either fights back and defends himself, or simply sits quietly, crushed.

It feels awful to hear this kind of feedback and just as bad to give it.

Then there are the managers who tell us they give plenty of "feedback," putting down their colleagues' work and pointing out flaws. "I'd rank the people I work with as a C, B– at best," one manager told us. "If I worked with smarter people, we'd get more things done around here. I tell them all the time what they need to do to improve, but it doesn't do anything." Meanwhile, private interviews with his colleagues revealed a team demotivated to the point of saying, "I'd rather quit than work for even another six months with that guy. It seems like I can't do anything right."

Skillful feedback, however, accelerates mastery. But again—it comes down to choice. A leader must intentionally create a culture that encourages feedback from all team members. And they have to own the choice to give performance-enhancing feedback every day.

On high-performing teams, colleagues give and receive insightful feedback daily. They know how to offer feedback that motivates performance and leads to improvement. They *mostly* give appreciative feedback. They rarely criticize or make people feel like they've done a bad job. When feedback *is* difficult to hear, these team members know how to share it constructively. When they receive difficult feedback themselves, they don't take it personally. We often hear team members say, "Working on this team makes me a lot better at what I do."

Bill Gates explains that feedback expertise is one of the key reasons the CEO of Microsoft, Satya Nadella, is so successful: "Satya has a natural ability to work well with lots of people, to tell people they're wrong in a nice way, and to let feedback come through to him more than I did. Microsoft's market cap is almost $600 billion, ahead of Facebook and Amazon by $100 billion. Not bad for a

41-year-old tech firm."[38] (As of the writing of this book, Microsoft's market cap is $2.1 trillion.)

Ask yourself this:

- ☐ "Would I be willing to completely change how I give and receive feedback if I could radically accelerate the performance of everyone on my team in a fraction of the time it took other leaders?"
- ☐ "Do people around me look forward to getting feedback?"
- ☐ "On a day-to-day basis, am I regularly getting feedback that immediately elevates my performance?"
- ☐ "On a scale of 1 to 10, is the quality of feedback I receive from my team a 9 or 10?"
- ☐ "When I give feedback, do I notice that my team members or others consistently respond with a tense or hostile pushback?"

If you are not receiving feedback on a daily or weekly basis that elevates your performance, or if you regularly experience hostile pushback when you *give* feedback, you've got room for improvement. Working on your team should always make you better at what you do. Otherwise, why be on a team? And those you work with should see you as a resource for their own improvement. If your feedback leads to defensiveness, demotivation, and resentments, your feedback isn't doing what you want it to.

But getting to the place where feedback elevates performance isn't just the responsibility of a team's manager. The whole team needs to put effort into establishing a feedback *culture*. You want feedback embedded in the DNA of your team: everyone gives it, and everyone expects it as a part of working together. When team members expect feedback as a regular team practice, this diffuses the fear of giving it and the resistance to hearing it.

To develop a strong feedback culture, everyone on the team needs to adopt a **coaching style of leadership**: the whole team gets better by giving each other feedback that leads to performance development. Think about professional athletes. They get feedback moment-to-moment on the practice court from coaches *and* teammates. Every day is devoted to getting and applying new, real-time information for improvement, a commitment critical for winning championships.

High-performing teams prioritize feedback the same way professional athletes do. Teammates seek it out from each other all the time. Team members trust each other, and when tough conversations arise, they draw from the strength of the shared Fundamental Why that bonds them together. They practice deep listening to understand each other's points of view. Because of the high level of trust in the team, people think about how their feedback supports each other's best interests. They give feedback that helps all of them move toward shared goals.

When you are a part of a high-performance team, you become coaches for one another's development. When you adopt a coaching style of leadership, you make each other better than you've ever been. It becomes your job to think of the best possible feedback you can give and trust that your teammates will do the same. You Give Feedback Like a Coach—the fourth practice of high-performance teams.

You commit to three disciplines to incorporate this practice:

1. Give strengths-based feedback.
2. Give solutions-oriented feedback.
3. Give constructive negative feedback.

We want to stress that your team can't reach peak performance unless *every member* participates in giving feedback. That means junior-level colleagues manage up by providing feedback to their bosses, and peer-to-peer feedback is the norm. This is unheard of in many work environments. We're used to our bosses giving primarily negative feedback a couple of times a year, and that's it. But just because that approach has been normalized doesn't mean it's the most effective way to improve. Rising above average means doing things most other teams won't do.

The only point of giving feedback to anyone, whether a direct report, a colleague, or even your manager, is to help them improve, right? So, regardless of who you're offering your feedback to, this approach can immediately improve performance and even feel good to give. The three feedback disciplines we share in this chapter are designed to help every team member, at every level, give daily feedback that actually enhances performance and is not uncomfortable, scary, or ego-bruising. Yes, such feedback exists. Top performers do it all the time.

1. Give Strengths-Based Feedback

We worked with one senior manager who had spent the early part of his career in a highly competitive market. (He described it as "cutthroat.") In this survival-of-the-fittest environment, he only received feedback when someone was disappointed, even angry. This is what he learned, so this is how he managed: quick to criticize, slow to praise.

But his current workplace had different values from his prior companies. His colleagues prided themselves on innovation and creativity. They intentionally created a healthier culture than the one he was used to. While he was a superstar at his job, he struggled as a manager. His direct reports told us in private they felt like nothing was ever good enough for him. No matter how hard they tried, it felt like they were failing. His team's motivation was low to average at best. Two team members told us they thought of quitting because of his management style.

When we first suggested he shift to **strengths-based feedback**, the manager was skeptical. He feared people would ease up unless he drove them hard. In addition, when we asked how each team member was performing individually, he had a whole list of complaints about what they were doing wrong. When we asked him what they did *right*, he said, "I'll have to take some time to think about that."

We asked him to do exactly that: make a list of each person on his team and write down what they were good at. Then we asked him to have a one-on-one meeting with each team member and give them *only* the appreciative feedback on the list. He did this once and said, "I gave the feedback, but there's still a lot for them to work on." So, we asked him to do it again in one month, and then again, once a month for three months. In addition to learning *how* to give strengths-based feedback, he had to work on *choosing* to make it a central part of how he communicates with his team.

After a few rounds of strengths-based feedback, something interesting happened: the manager started *noticing* more of what his team members did well. He also observed higher engagement on the team. After a few months, everyone we interviewed confirmed that he seemed like a different person. They actually enjoyed working with him. After six months, the manager told us his team's performance was at an all-time high.

People are so unaccustomed to doing this, but it's remarkable what happens when you start to focus on strengths-based feedback. It's not just a technique; it's a cultural shift that shuts down negativity bias. When you focus on what's working, more starts to work. It's a cause-and-effect principle that may seem counterintuitive until you do it.

The manager in our story had no idea he was actually in the way of his team's performance. When a manager only criticizes, it's a self-fulfilling prophecy. It creates a team that does things just to avoid negativity instead of stepping forward with more of what's working.

To shift from low-performing to high-performing, it's vital to give feedback you believe will improve performance. This is a judgment call. If you are not sure, ask yourself:

"How will this feedback improve this person's performance?"

What kind of feedback improves performance? According to the HBR study mentioned at the beginning of this chapter, focusing on strengths is key. As a bonus, strengths-based feedback also enhances employee engagement. Gallup found that "a vast majority (67%) of employees who strongly agree that their manager focuses on their strengths or positive characteristics are engaged, compared with 31% of employees who strongly agree that their manager focuses on their weaknesses."[39]

Strengths-based feedback builds strengths. What you focus on, you create.

We first learned this from one of the pioneering books on the field of high performance, *The Inner Game of Tennis* by W. Timothy Gallwey. Gallwey was a tennis coach back in the 70s who'd grown up learning the old way of giving critical feedback to tennis players. But as he matured in his coaching career, he discovered something profound. The more he would tell someone *not* to swing the racket that way or hit the ball like that, the more the player would struggle. Gallwey's constant corrections threw the player off her game.

Gallwey pointed out that critical feedback interfered with the player's ability to access peak performance. It puts the player "in her head," *thinking* about what not to do. Instead, Gallwey had his players focus on building from the things they could already do well, bypassing the critical mental chatter and quickly improving their game. Gallwey helped athletes achieve all of the radical changes we mentioned at the beginning of this chapter. He could take a seemingly clumsy, unathletic person who others might write off as hopeless, and within a few hours, they were volleying tennis balls back and forth.[40] When you focus on what you already do well, you get immersed in doing the action—so much so that thoughts disappear. As a result, the skill builds more quickly.

In his book *Flow*, psychologist Mihaly Csikszentmihalyi calls this the **flow state**. In this peak performance state, Csikszentmihalyi says, "Time flies. Every action, movement, and thought follows inevitably from the previous one, like playing jazz. Your whole being is involved, and you're using your skills to the utmost."[41] When athletes, stage performers, mountain climbers, creative workers, and leaders are in a flow state, it's as if time disappears. Their capabilities expand—almost like magic—and they can operate at peak performance.

Have you had the experience of being so immersed in your work that hours pass by without you noticing? Many of the teams we work with describe their meetings this way. They collectively enter the flow state. As a tennis coach, Gallwey found that "don't do that" feedback inhibited a player's ability to enter the flow state. The same is true for your team. When team members criticize each other, tension, friction, and disengagement dominate. For this reason, *high-performance feedback does not focus on "what is not working."* Instead, we recommend focusing primarily on what *is* working, supporting your team's ability to collaborate in a state of peak-performance flow.

To do this requires a shift in thinking for teams considering feedback a bad thing. Remember, feedback is simply "information that leads to improvement." When you give feedback well, your teammates will welcome your input. Strengths-based feedback feels good *and* helps the people you work with improve. Like great athletic coaches, teams and their managers should prioritize providing regular, affirming feedback about what they like and want to see more of. Less criticism brings fewer fight/flight/freeze incidents and more receptivity to constructive suggestions. When team members don't need to be hypervigilant, they relax more, and their ability to learn new skills increases.

Don't mistake strengths-based feedback as a mere exercise to make people feel better. Strengths-based feedback is about giving performance-enhancing information all day long. Reinforcing specific behaviors or achievements leads to producing more of these behaviors and achievements. By hearing "good pass," a basketball point guard receives information to pass like that again. She can more easily do it again because she's focused on what she did well.

On lower-performing teams, examples of strengths-based feedback are few and far between. People on lower-performing teams have told us, "I come to work every day having no idea if I'm going to get fired." These employees receive little to no affirming feedback, so what other conclusion can they come to? Surprisingly, the boss might tell us the employee is doing great, but he failed to communicate this to the employee. Or when the manager *does* give strengths-based feedback, it's just to cushion the blow of the critical, negative feedback that comes next.

> For these reasons, we ask everyone we work with to practice ongoing, strengths-based feedback. This discipline is simple. It looks like this:
>
> 1. You say:
>   - ☐ "Here is what is working…"
>   - ☐ "Here is what is going well…"
>   - ☐ "What you are doing well is…"
> 2. Give *specific* examples of exactly what is working.
> 3. Add a "Nice job" and "Thank you."
> 4. Practice this all day, every day.

Step 4 can seem unrealistic if you're brand new to this. But just try it. Sometimes it can be as simple as, "This is excellent, thank you," when a colleague delivers great work.

Other times daily feedback is more specific. Our executive assistant, Christel, helped Justin improve how he assigns tasks using strengths-based feedback during everyday interactions. Recently Justin asked Christel to draft three different survey options for a client project. He said, "I want to run an experiment to see if the results vary based on how the survey's questions are ordered and worded. I'd like this because I want to show the objectivity of our survey, but also allow the client to make choices based on what they want to learn. Can you please create three options by Thursday, so we can review them in time for our client meeting on Monday?"

Afterward, Christel shared that she appreciated the clarity of instructions Justin had given her. "I love how specific this request was," she said. "I love how you included the Fundamental Why, and you gave me a 'by when.' The 'by when' really helps me prioritize my workload."

Moving forward, Justin became more intentional about including this level of specificity regarding the Fundamental Why of his request, and a "by when." These are both practices he knows are important. He hadn't realized he let them slip in the busyness of his heavy workload. Christel's strengths-based feedback helped reorient him toward better leadership habits. We all fall out of practice; that's why feedback from those you manage is so crucial.

Once you adopt the practice, it sparks a mindset shift that perpetuates high performance. We worked with two co-founders recently whose mindset was locked in negativity bias. All day, every day, they operated from a place of concern, trying to anticipate what could go wrong. They were constantly tense. We helped them break the cycle by focusing on strengths-based feedback. It took a lot of effort, no doubt. They had to choose to focus on what was working and make it a daily practice. But once they did this for a while, they described it as wizardry or magic.

It's not magic. It's a proven tool for high performance. This doesn't mean difficult conversations don't happen. We'll show you how to give critical feedback in just a minute. But when strengths-based feedback is your baseline, the hard discussions become easier because everyone on your team operates in a culture of feedback.

2. Give Solutions-Oriented Feedback

At this point, you might be thinking, "Okay, great. We give more affirming feedback about what's going well, but there are still things we need to improve on, aren't there? You can't just ignore those."

Once again, feedback is "information that leads to improvement." If there are areas for improvement, you must give the right information.

Think of coaches on the ballfield. They are constantly affirming, "Nice pitch." But they still give regular, ongoing, directional suggestions for improvement. "Shorten your stance a little on this next one," or "Try dropping back a bit."

Ongoing **solutions-oriented feedback** supports the development of the player in action. This means giving clear, ongoing suggestions for improvement. This does not mean demanding that everybody do what you think they should. Instead, make regular suggestions and offer feedback as a helpful perspective to try, rather than a prescription for what to do. When you establish this as a team practice, regular feedback is welcomed and encouraged as a way of working together.

Engineers and product developers are familiar with ongoing feedback for product development innovations. They have learned "Design Thinking" (prototype > test > feedback > iterate) or "Minimum Viable Product (MVP)" approaches to innovation that rely on constant feedback. In the same way, high-performing teams apply this level of ongoing feedback to *all* aspects of their work together—including individual and team performance—to ensure they are adapting to real-time shifts and changes.

But ongoing feedback needs to lead to improvement. The feedback needs to be specific and clear, and support the *improvement* of a person and their work. Ongoing criticism we typically hear on lower-performing teams starts with phrases like, "I don't really like what you did here," or, "Something about this is off," or, "Fix this." This type of feedback communicates that something is wrong but leaves the recipient wondering what to do about it.

One manager we work with told us he got feedback from his executive boss, who told him, "I don't like the way you are showing up in meetings." When the manager asked what he could do about it, the executive said, "I don't know. It's just feedback. Do what you will with it." Without specific areas to focus on, the manager was left confused and dejected. Feedback like this can impair performance rather than improve it.

Solutions-oriented feedback, on the other hand, offers clear suggestions and builds on what's already working. As importantly, you give the Fundamental Why of your feedback. When recipients of feedback understand your Fundamental Why, they may follow your suggestions to the letter or innovate an even better solution on their own. In our example with Justin and Christel, the Fundamental Why of her feedback was, "the 'by when' really helps me prioritize my workload." Knowing this gave Justin a concrete reason to keep doing what was working.

To determine the specific solutions-oriented feedback you want to offer, consider what supports your goals, the team goals, and the recipient's goals.

Before speaking with the feedback recipient, answer the questions:

- ☐ "What specific feedback would move this person toward our goals?"
- ☐ "What strengths can they build on? What do I like about what they are doing?"
- ☐ "What suggestions can I see that they might not yet see?"
- ☐ "Considering the Fundamental Why of the project, what specific actions would support achieving this intention?"

Start with what's working and always be specific and direct.

Here is the basic structure for giving solutions-oriented feedback:

1. Start with strengths-based feedback. "Here is what is going (or went) well…" [followed by specifics]
2. Add solutions-oriented suggestions, beginning with "From my perspective…"
   - ☐ "From my perspective, one thing you might try is…"
   - ☐ "From my perspective, some suggested improvements you might work with could be…"
   - ☐ "From my perspective, it would be even better if…"
3. Give specific suggestions.

4. State the Fundamental Why of your suggestions. When someone understands why you are making the suggestions, they can adapt your guidance to their specific work.

☐ "I think this will simplify the user's end experience..."

☐ "I think this can help the client understand why we're unable to budge on these costs..."

☐ "I think this will help optimize cash flow over the course of three months..."

5. Ask:

☐ "What do you think?"

At this point, you might be thinking, "Won't the person feel set up when you start with what's working? Waiting for the other shoe to drop?"

Not if you pay attention to precisely how solutions-oriented feedback is delivered. Notice how the feedback is suggestive. Notice also that you start each piece of suggestive feedback with "From my perspective." All feedback *is* from your own perspective. It's not right or wrong, but a point of view for the other person to consider. And finally, notice how the feedback concludes with a request for input from the recipient. This request indicates you are willing to listen to the person's perspective and be open to their point of view.

For instance, "[Strengths-based] Here's what went well: Your presentation was beautifully designed and well-organized. I think everyone in the room was impressed and confident we've got our stuff together. Nice job with that; great presentation! [Solutions-oriented] From my perspective, it would be even better if the executive team saw this presentation. To get it ready for them, I'd suggest tightening up the copy to just one to three bullets per slide. [Fundamental Why] The executives are thinking about ten things at once, and I think that's all the bandwidth they have to pay attention to. What do you think?"

Notice the key elements here:

- ☐ It started with what went well.
- ☐ The solutions-oriented feedback started with "From my perspective."
- ☐ There is a clear Fundamental Why.
- ☐ It turns into a dialog by asking, "What do you think?"

When an entire team starts practicing solutions-oriented feedback with each other, we quickly see improvements in team productivity, performance, and mood. People's faces look brighter the next time we see them!

Sometimes, a project or leader may simply need a more condensed version of solutions-oriented feedback. The condensed version can look like this:

1. "What's working is..."
2. "From my perspective, it would be even better if..."

One final note: sometimes you might see a teammate's work and want to criticize it. You wonder why the individual would have chosen to approach a project that way. *Keep in mind that the judgment you hold about an individual's work is your own point of view.* You simply see things differently. That doesn't mean the other person is wrong—they just don't see what you see. When this happens, it requires a certain level of **self-awareness** to reframe your criticism into a piece of feedback that works. Rather than jump to criticize, start by assuming the individual had good intentions. Then focus on giving constructive feedback that will lead to improvement.

3. Give Constructive Negative Feedback

When teams practice strengths-based and solutions-oriented feedback, we might hear a manager say, "I'm giving far more appreciative, strengths-based feedback. We're doing solutions-oriented feedback on our team, and we're finally moving forward on some projects that have stalled for a long time. But sometimes, there really *is* an issue that needs to be addressed specifically, like when a team member is clearly not pulling their weight. Or dropping a lot of balls. Or being a jerk. What do I do then?"

Sometimes, you *do* need to deliver hard truths about someone's performance, a truth that will be difficult to hear. There's no getting around this. In *Radical Candor*, Kim Malone Scott says. "It's brutally hard to tell people when they are screwing up. You don't want to hurt anyone's feelings; that's because you're not a sadist. You don't want that person or the rest of the team to think you're a jerk. Plus, you've been told since you learned to talk, 'If you don't have anything nice to say, don't say anything at all.' Now, all of a sudden, it's your job to say it. You've got to undo a lifetime of training."[2]

High-performing teams can exchange more honest feedback than their lower-performing counterparts. They can give more pointed, **constructive negative feedback** because they have done the work of learning each other's Fundamental Why, building trust, listening to understand, and giving mostly strengths-based or solutions-oriented feedback.

Whole Foods CEO John Mackey sums it up well: "If you (give) enough positive reinforcement, people are going to be in a place where they can receive the critical feedback. That gives you permission to give negative feedback." In this same interview, he emphasized the importance of establishing trust to be able to do this, saying, "Criticism will only be received by people if there's a high degree of trust. If there's trust, and people know that you care about them, then their self-esteem is less threatened."[43]

In other words, the trust and camaraderie built among a higher-performance team support a "high-heat" conversation. Higher-performing teams have a foundation of trust that allows them to tell each other the *truth*. They rely on each other to help them course correct. In fact, they *expect it*.

One CEO we worked with spent an entire day with a piece of broccoli stuck in her teeth. Finally, in a meeting at the end of the day, someone told her.

She exclaimed, "How come no one told me I have broccoli in my teeth?"

One teammate shrugged and said, "We didn't want to embarrass you."

Even though this was a light-hearted situation, the CEO expressed concern. "If you don't tell me I've got broccoli in my teeth because you don't want to embarrass me, what else are you not telling me? You're my team. I want to hear all the feedback: good, bad, and ugly. I need to hear it. That's what makes me better."

Of course, most constructive negative feedback is more challenging to hear than broccoli in your teeth. But high-performance team players want to hear everything—even the hard stuff. They rely on feedback to improve. No one loves to hear how they're underperforming, upsetting others, or detracting from the team. But, if you see it, the person needs to hear it. If you don't provide feedback, the individual will never be able to course correct.

Always remember, if feedback doesn't improve performance, it's not really feedback. It's just bad news. *How* you give feedback matters. *Always try to turn negative feedback into a conversation.* In this conversation, share your exact perception about the issue and help the individual create a path forward. By the end of the conversation, the feedback recipient should be clear about specific actions that will lead to improvement *and can help come up with the solution.* That's what makes this *constructive* negative feedback. Like a good coach, your feedback should empower the recipient to grow and improve on their own.

We also recommend giving up broad generalizations altogether. Be specific about what you see isn't working. Ask what they think. Ask them for their input first before you share your solutions. Start with questions like:

"Do you know what I am talking about?"

"What do you think could be some ways to improve?"

Because these difficult feedback moments require great skill, it's important to consider what you want to say, how you want to say it, and why you need to say it. You also want to balance empathy for the person's feelings with the willingness to give it to them straight. Offer clear, concrete examples of what you're observing. When the person responds to your feedback, don't rush to defend your position. Practice deep listening throughout.

Here is the format we use to give constructive negative feedback:

1. "What's going well is..." (be specific).
2. *"One* thing that has been in the way is _____" (focus only on one thing at a time).
3. Share specific instances so the person can relate to a particular time you are referring to in your feedback. Mention:
   - ☐ *When*: When did this happen, and what was the context?
   - ☐ What: What specifically they did
   - ☐ Effect: The effect that this behavior had on the situation and why it was detrimental
   - ☐ In practice, it sounds like this: "When _____ you did _____ and then _____ happened."
   - ☐ If there are multiple situations, you can cite more than one. Always ground the feedback in specific examples. *The more specific you can be, the better.*
4. Ask: "Have you noticed this? Do you know what I'm talking about? Do you have thoughts about this?"
5. Ask: "What do you think some solutions could be? What actions do you want to take?"
6. [If you have additional suggestions] Ask: "Are you open to a few suggestions?"
   - ☐ "From my perspective, some suggested improvements would be _____" (Offer

> a possible way to improve or solve, *always*
> starting with "From my perspective.")
>
> 7. Ask: "Are these helpful?"

Here is an example of giving constructive negative feedback using the above format:

Hey John, I wanted to talk with you about something. Lately, you've been writing some excellent copy. The writing is clear and crisp. It's some of the best work you've done yet. From my perspective, I've also noticed that you seem unhappy with a couple of people on our team. The other day during our production meeting, when you were responding to Jason, you got loud and talked over Jason when he started to speak. It seemed like you were angry. Then the rest of the meeting got sidetracked to focus on resolving your concern. Others on the team seemed to check out after that happened. This happened twice before in production meetings. Do you know what I am talking about? Do you have any thoughts about that situation?

At this point in the conversation, John might get defensive and justify his point of view. *Practice deep listening!* Make sure you repeat back his point of view and that you thoroughly understand his Fundamental Why. When he acknowledges that you understand where he is coming from, ask if he has any thoughts about actions he could take. (Side note: When your team has done the work to build trust through deep listening, John will probably be less defensive. These conversations will go much more smoothly.)

In this case, let's say John understands the issue, but can't think of how to make a shift. You ask: "Are you open to suggestions?" If yes, you could say:

> From my perspective, one suggestion for improvement would be to provide more strengths-based feedback with suggested solutions in meetings rather than focusing on what's wrong. I'd also suggest you practice deep listening rather than talking over someone. When you get upset and criticize, it shuts others down. You make a lot of good points, but they aren't taken in well by the rest of the team. I think a shift in your communication style would come across better to the team. What do you think about that idea? Do you have any additional ideas? What are you willing to do differently in the future?

While this kind of feedback is difficult, turning negative feedback into a conversation for growth allows it to be constructive. You are not *telling* a team member how to behave. Instead, you are asking for input on what he thinks he could do differently and what he is willing to do. It takes courage to approach feedback in this way, but when practiced as a team, the discipline becomes the norm.

Always remember, every person you work with is a human being. Receiving negative feedback stings, especially when someone's work is a big part of how they find value in the world. Make sure your feedback is always in the recipient's best interest. When giving and receiving feedback, speak in a way that shows you care. Be empathetic. Practice what *The Culture Code's* Daniel Coyle calls "belonging cues"—behaviors that create a sense of safe connection, like eye contact, good energy, taking turns speaking and listening, paying attention, friendly body language, and a warm tone.[44] And *always* give difficult negative feedback in person, never in an email or text.

Bottom line: any time you give feedback, treat people with care, dignity, and respect.

ASK FOR FEEDBACK—ABOUT YOURSELF

We once worked with a senior director of IT at a large company. She had been dealing with complaints from her team for years about a cross-departmental conflict with the customer service department. From her perspective, customer service made incessant, unreasonable demands. Customer service personnel would ask for one thing and completely change their minds about what they needed after IT fulfilled the initial request. The IT director's team was at their wit's end.

We suggested she cross company lines and get feedback from the customer service perspective. The objective was not to resolve anything, argue with customer service, or defend her team. We were merely suggesting she learn a different perspective.

She sat down with three other department leaders and asked for straightforward feedback. She did not defend her team. She just wanted to know, from the other department's perspective, how was IT doing?

When she came back after these interviews, she was blown away. "All these years, I've only been listening to my own team. They convinced me the problem was the other department. That's all I ever heard. In these feedback sessions, I heard a completely different story. We aren't giving them what they really ask for. We give them what we want to give them. They shared some stories about how intimidated they feel making requests because of how stubborn my guys are when they approach us. I had no idea it was like this, and I can see what to do differently now. This exercise also helped me connect with the managers over there in a completely new way. When the meetings started, they seemed defensive. By the time each of these interviews was over, though, we shook hands with a feeling of partnership we've never had. We've agreed to do this exercise together every three months."

While the changes the director had to make as a result of her findings weren't easy, the two teams began working well together for the first time in years. Without those feedback interviews, however, that silo division may have continued indefinitely.

These types of feedback meetings are called **feedback listening tours**: one-on-one interviews conducted to gather feedback, insight, and information. In a feedback listening tour, the person asking for feedback is there to *listen*, not to debate or solve problems on the spot.

One CEO we work with conducts feedback listening tours monthly. As soon as something is amiss on his executive team, he asks for feedback about what he can do differently. When he sees a challenge in specific departments, he interviews the directors and managers to learn more about what he and the executive team can do about it. He also sets the expectation that his executive team does the same with their direct reports. Over the past eight years, his company was hit with multiple economic setbacks, and each time, he conducted listening tours with his clients to get feedback. Recently, the company he started eight years prior was sold to a top technology company for many times its revenue.

To expose oneself to honest feedback takes humility and courage: receiving feedback requires you to leave your ego at the door.

But by *asking* for feedback, you're no longer operating in the vacuum of your own perceptions. You gain previously unknown information that allows you to make changes fast. Jim Yong Kim, Former President of the World Bank, put it this way: "No matter how good you think you are as a leader, my goodness, the people around you will have all kinds of ideas for how you can get better. So, for me, the most fundamental thing about leadership is to have the humility to continue to get feedback and to try to get better—because your job is to try to help everybody else get better."[45]

As you build your team feedback culture, nothing has more impact than a manager asking for feedback *about themselves*. In their book *No Rules Rules*, Erin Meyer and Netflix co-founder Reed Hastings say, "You might think that the first step for cultivating candor would be to begin with what's easiest: having the boss give copious feedback to her staff. I recommend instead focusing first on something much more difficult: getting employees to give candid feedback to the boss."[46]

Most people on lower-performing teams have never once had a manager ask them for feedback about their performance as a leader. But where the leader goes, the team follows. When a manager is vulnerable enough to ask for feedback, it builds the kind of vulnerability-based trust we explored in Practice 2. By modeling your own willingness to receive feedback as a manager, you set the tone for a team culture where others welcome feedback. Plus, as a manager, no one in the world can give you better feedback about how you lead than the people who work for you.

For this reason, we recommend managers do feedback listening tours regularly with each of their direct reports. But listening tours are not just for managers! Everyone on a team should do this with each other *and* with members of cross-functional teams. When team members ask each other for feedback on a regular basis, it lessens the tension around difficult conversations. These teams are more open with each other about the truth. When team members conduct feedback interviews with cross-functional team members, this dissolves the "us vs. them" mentality so often plaguing company silos. In all instances, regular feedback interviews provide essential, real-time information that leads to improvement.

It's essential that these are dedicated meetings. As you cultivate a feedback culture, people won't approach listening tours with the same dread they bring to traditional performance reviews. In this case, the person getting the feedback requests the meeting, which fosters the exact opposite vibe of a scheduled performance review. The person getting the feedback is inviting it as an act of leadership, because they want to hear what will help them improve.

Here is how to conduct a feedback interview:

1. Schedule a full sixty minutes for a one-on-one conversation. Anonymous "360s" are never sufficient replacements for this conversation.
2. During this meeting, ask specific questions about your performance. If you are conducting a cross-functional feedback interview, ask about your team or department's performance as well. Here are a few sample questions to consider:
   ☐ From your perspective, what am I doing well as a leader? What is my team/department doing well?
   ☐ From your perspective, what could I do better? What could my team/department do better?

☐ What advice do you have for me? What advice do you have for my team?

☐ What is possible for us in our work together if we were wildly successful?

☐ [We recommend always ending with this last question. It builds partnership and ensures that the feedback given supports furthering progress together.]

3. Practice deep listening when receiving feedback. Do NOT argue or defend. This will completely shut down another person. Repeat back what you hear, ask inquiring questions, and simply say, "Thank you."

Apply what you learn! You won't always agree with the feedback you receive. But if you listen for the Fundamental Why and ask yourself, "why was this feedback important to the person giving it to me?" you'll find creative ways to apply what you hear. Once you apply a piece of feedback you received from someone, find time to share with them exactly what you applied and how it worked. By doing this, you let your team know that you not only ask for feedback but also apply it.

We often work with fifty or sixty executives, directors, and managers in a workshop setting. During these workshops, we have managers conduct feedback listening tours with each other. Afterward, we often hear, "That was some of the best feedback I've received in my life." We then have all workshop participants go out and do listening tours across the company.

The effect is immediately palpable, almost as if the organization sees with new eyes. In a matter of days, a critical mass of the organization's leaders has insight into areas they can improve upon. When they put this feedback into action, their culture experiences a jolt in performance. It can happen for you, too, if every team member commits to conducting feedback listening tours regularly.

At first, this discipline can sting: it takes great humility to accept feedback, particularly from people who work for you. But it can also become one of the most important practices you take on in your career. When your entire team regularly solicits feedback from each other and the people they work with cross-functionally, your entire team culture can transform in days. (Yes, it is that powerful.)

Finally, it requires courage, humility, and vulnerability to ask for feedback—and to give it. Teams that do this at the highest levels commit to receiving feedback with the grace of professionals who know feedback makes them better. How you receive feedback makes or breaks this practice. As Kim Scott says in *Radical Candor*, "The way you ask for criticism and react when you get it goes a long way toward building trust—or destroying it."[47] Arguing, pushing back, or dismissing feedback you receive denigrates the entire feedback culture you and your team are working so hard to build. When you respond to feedback with appreciation, no matter how difficult it is to hear, you exhibit a crucial skill of great leadership. This is the kind of leadership that high-performance teams are built upon.

To summarize, high-performing teams mostly give each other **strengths-based feedback**: specific, appreciative feedback that focuses on what's going well. They often support this with **solutions-oriented feedback**: feedback that offers specific suggestions for improvement that builds upon strengths. They selectively give **constructive negative feedback** through one-on-one dialog that empowers the person receiving the feedback. To ensure that the team prioritizes giving *and* receiving feedback as part of their team's culture, everyone, including the manager, regularly *asks for feedback about themselves.*

From our observation, teams that Give Feedback Like a Coach are rare, but some of the highest-performing. Team members get fired up whenever they get together. There's a lot more, "I really liked how you..." or, "Nice job on that..." or, "Here's what I liked about that..." These team members often tell others outside the team about the strengths of their teammates. People on these teams describe an environment where they get in the flow together, time seems to disappear, and creativity, focus, passion, and inspiration take over.

The practice in this chapter can get your teams there, too.

PRACTICE FOUR

GIVE FEEDBACK LIKE A COACH

STRUCTURE FOR APPLICATION

1. As a team, commit to the practice of giving and receiving feedback (i.e., information that leads to improvement) on a day-to-day basis.

2. All day, every day, offer specific feedback about "what is going well." Include affirmations like "nice job" and "thank you." Usually, this affirmative feedback is enough.

3. As needed, give solutions-oriented suggestive feedback. Always begin with "From my perspective..."

4. When necessary, give more difficult, direct feedback about areas that need specific changes by providing concrete examples (i.e., when...you did...then this happened...). Be considerate in both speaking and listening; pay attention to the person you are speaking with; have friendly body language; and use a warm tone. *Always* give difficult negative feedback in person, never in an email or text.

5. Turn difficult feedback into a dialog by asking, "What do you think? What do you see could be ways to address this issue?"

6. Anytime you have a difficult challenge with other team members, practice asking for feedback. Conduct feedback listening tours with your direct reports and everyone you work with.

7. Practice care, dignity, and respect whenever you give feedback.

ADAPT YOUR WORK STYLE

"The strength of the team is each individual member.
The strength of each member is the team."
—PHIL JACKSON, Six-Time National Champion NBA Coach

Conflicting work styles get in the way of collaboration. A visionary CEO tells us the director of technology overwhelms her with too much information. In turn, the director of technology tells us the CEO moves too fast. The human resources director tells us the COO is cold and too process-oriented. But when we talk to the COO, she says the HR director doesn't plan far enough ahead to get things done. In these scenarios, people are frustrated with each other because their work styles are diametrically opposed. Their communication is poor (sometimes bordering on toxic), but no one knows what to do about it. They judge each other harshly, and nobody knows how to get what they want.

How can a team work well together when its individual members are so *different* from each other?

To reach peak performance, teammates must adapt their work style preferences to complement—and sometimes match—those of the other team members. In doing so, you'll discover strengths where you previously saw none, and your own work style will become more fluid, agile, and receptive to new ways of thinking.

Doing this takes buy-in from the team. Everyone must agree to adapt their work styles, depending on whom they work with. This requires seeing your differences as strengths instead of obstacles, and learning how to draw from those strengths. Adapting your work style to embrace other people's strengths requires everybody to learn how to *communicate* differently, which isn't always easy.

But it's worth doing. According to the 2011 Holmes Report, productivity takes a $47 billion hit each year in US and UK businesses due to poor communications, which equals a loss of $26,041 per worker. On the flip side, leaders who are effective communicators produce 47 percent higher shareholder returns than those who aren't.[48]

On lower-performing teams, poor communication causes stress, and meetings are unproductive. Individuals communicate the way they always have, with little or no regard for the impact of their preferred style on everybody else. People get annoyed with each other and leave meetings thinking, "What a waste of time."

High-performing teams have a markedly different experience. Team members learn to adapt their work styles and recognize each other's strengths. They rely on each other to close the gaps in areas where they aren't as strong. They know how to adjust presentation and speaking styles depending upon who is in the room. They take full responsibility for adapting their own communication preferences to accommodate whomever they're working with. People on high-performing teams learn how to shift and adapt their preferred work styles to meet others where they are.

High-performing teammates change *themselves* rather than assume everybody else should be different.

One CEO once asked us, "Can you just teach my team how to talk to me?" As much as you might prefer other people to adapt to you first, it's not likely—especially without the right team practice in place. As a leader, it's your responsibility to figure out how to work with *them*, which means *you* must Adapt *Your* Work Style. This sets an example and an expectation. Then, when the team follows suit and adapts their own work styles, a natural collaboration emerges.

Take it upon yourself to observe, understand, and adapt to styles other than your own. If your goal is to be understood, how you speak, the questions you ask, and how you present information should be modified to accommodate your audience.

The practice in this chapter will show you how to adapt your own style, and will give your teammates the foundation to adapt theirs. You may be surprised by how easy this practice becomes once you understand how it works. By using a basic tool to assess someone's work style, your team can quickly adapt to make sure effective communication takes place.

LEARN EACH OTHER'S WORK STYLES USING THE TILT

We recommend using a personality-based assessment to understand individual work styles and adapt accordingly. Personality assessments are useful because they provide insights into how people think and act based on who they are. We've found that the most effective personality assessment for practical application on work teams is the TILT 365 assessment (or "TILT") developed by Pam Boney, an executive coach with a background in industrial/organizational psychology. (For more information or to take the TILT, visit TILT365.com.) We recommend that everyone in your organization take this assessment.

In our experience, the TILT most clearly defines the four basic work styles we encounter on almost every team. The TILT is particularly instructive for learning how to work with each other, which is why it has been used by fast-moving, innovative organizations like Clif Bar, Facebook, and Red Hat.

The assessment is often so accurate that we hear people say, "How does it know me so well?" They're fascinated by what they learn about themselves from the in-depth report, which provides a significant amount of learning for personal growth and how to apply it. Many of our clients have even shared that knowing their TILT profile (and their spouse's) has made their marriages better!

You can experience the benefits of the TILT as soon as you learn it. On one senior leadership team we worked with, the five members of the team had distinctly different working styles. The CEO loved talking about big ideas and possibilities. This frustrated the COO; he thought the CEO was wasting time on ideas that weren't rooted in reality. Some people wanted to implement the ideas right away, and others wanted to move more cautiously. When we interviewed the team, they shared how frustrated they were with each other. The situation had gotten impossible to deal with, and their meetings were completely stalled.

As soon as we showed these executives the four types of work styles, eyes grew wide. (A couple of them even laughed.) Right away, the team realized they were at odds with each other largely because they each had different preferred work styles. Without realizing it, they experienced the others' differing work styles as "weak." Immediately following their TILT assessments, the team began to adapt their styles and became more open to drawing on each other's strengths. They also became less insistent that others were doing things wrong.

The COO, for Instance, realized that the CEO's visionary nature was equally as important as the details of how they were going to get there. Sometimes, when the CEO would talk about the "next big thing," the COO felt it was out of touch with what they needed to do now. But without the CEO's big-picture thinking, the COO was at risk of getting stuck in details and processes. Instead of seeing their contrasting styles as a weakness, they both realized they needed each other's preferred work styles to benefit the team: the big picture *and* the details. Following this discussion on their different TILT styles, team meetings shifted from tension to collaboration.

It's important to understand that taking the TILT assessment is not the same as applying the TILT model. It takes practice to incorporate what you've learned. Knowing what your differences are doesn't tell you how to accommodate them. By applying the TILT model explored in this chapter—with consistency and over time—you will resolve a significant number of barriers and stressors on your team. Even if you've never taken the assessment, just learning the basics in this chapter will quickly enhance your team's ability to collaborate.

IDENTIFY YOUR STRENGTHS AND
WEAKNESSES USING THE TILT

While the TILT assessment is a rich, in-depth exploration of different styles at work, we find it useful because it's built on a straightforward framework. All you need to remember are these four distinct styles: *impact, connection, clarity*, and *structure*. We've found that these four styles allow people of diverse backgrounds and work styles to quickly work together on any team (including cross-functional teams where people don't always know each other well).

The basic TILT model we adapted from the TILT 365 assessment is shown on the following page.

In the TILT model shown, we see the four primary styles, each having its own strengths and challenges. It's called the TILT model because both people and teams naturally TILT toward certain styles. Usually, a team TILTs toward the style most comfortable to the manager or the style most team members share. But no one's style is fixed. With practice, individuals and teams can choose to TILT toward other styles, not just their own. Collaboration, innovation, and productivity increase when a team learns to TILT toward all four styles.

By reflecting on how you communicate, you can quickly figure out how you TILT.

If you're an **impact-oriented person**, you talk a lot about the big picture. You want to set big goals and talk about results. You get excited when conversations turn to possibilities. You prefer three bullet points as opposed to an in-depth report, and you tune out when a discussion gets bogged down by detail. *Sometimes you act like you know everything and dominate conversations when you get stressed.*

TILT STRENGTHS QUADRANTS

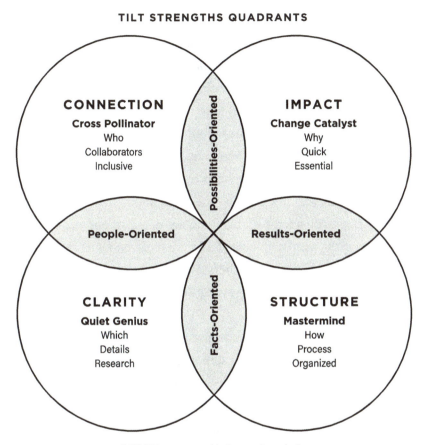

IMPACT focuses on achieving results and why.

CONNECTION focuses on ensuring people are doing well, and everyone
stays connected with each other and to big possibilities.

CLARITY focuses on the data and details, generating clarity to make strong decisions.

STRUCTURE focuses on structural processes and procedures about how to get results.

A **connection-oriented person** talks a lot about people, big
ideas, and feelings. If you skew toward connection, you socialize
ideas across the organization and make sure everyone is looped into
your communications. You like to introduce people to each other
because you know who needs what the other person has to offer.

You like talking about who knows whom and how people are feeling. You advocate for people in meetings and push against ideas if they aren't considering people first. *Sometimes you can seem checked out or "absent in the room" when things get too stressful.*

A **clarity-oriented person** cites research when they bring forward an idea. If you are clarity-oriented, you are thorough in your reporting and presentations. You present *all* the facts and push back when not enough details have been considered. You can be slow to make decisions and ask a lot of questions about small things others might not consider. Although you are detail-oriented, you also think about the people involved and want to do enough research to make the best decisions for others. *When you get stressed, you move into "analysis paralysis" and get agitated by having to make decisions without more information.*

A **structure-oriented person** is the process planner and architect. They usually present each step of a plan in their presentations. If you are a structure-oriented person, you are practical in how you talk and don't want to spend much time talking about how people feel. When people present ideas, you're the one asking, "How are you going to do that?" *When you get stressed out, you attempt to micromanage the process, which can make teammates feel stifled by you.*

All four styles create a well-balanced team. Once you understand how you TILT—and how you *don't* TILT—you will begin to recognize strengths in styles other than your own.

But what makes the TILT especially helpful is that it doesn't claim all individuals have a fixed TILT. The model is agile, since people are, too. The model also provides immediate insight into which strengths to work on.

SHIFT YOUR STYLE

It's a logical conclusion that strong teams exhibit attributes from all four work styles. You want the impact's vision and push for results *as well as* the rigorous attention to detail that clarity brings. You want the Connector's emphasis on socializing ideas and including the right people *as well as* the structure-oriented person's well-thought-out plan.

But let's be honest. You don't always see strengths in some of these styles, do you?

Usually, the style diagonally across from yours on the TILT quadrant (as previously shown) is the hardest for you to adapt to.

Let's say you're a fast-moving impact person. When a clarity-oriented person slogs through never-ending details, you get annoyed and frustrated. You've probably thought to yourself, "Why are they slowing everything down? Let's just make a decision and get on with it."

And if you're more clarity-oriented, that same impact person has you clutching your seat when they seem to skip over necessary details and make decisions without thinking everything through. "It's never going to work. They're not paying attention to what we need," you think. You even feel your body tense up.

If you're a connection-oriented person, you've often wondered why the structure-oriented planner always seems so serious. "Why can't they lighten up a little," you think to yourself.

On the other hand, if you're a structure-oriented person, you might think a connection person is wasting time talking about things that don't matter. "These meetings would be a lot shorter if we didn't have to talk so much. Can we please just cut to the chase and move on?" As one structure-oriented director of operations light-heartedly remarked during a trust-building exercise, "I don't really care how you feel."

To create a more agile team, everyone needs to accept that differences aren't a problem—they're an asset. But to appreciate your team's strengths requires a high level of **self-awareness**: a willingness to take an honest look at yourself first.

A 2013 *Forbes* research study on what makes leaders successful found that "a high self-awareness score was the strongest predictor of overall success. This is not altogether surprising as executives aware of their weaknesses are often better able to hire subordinates who perform well in categories in which the leader lacks acumen."[49] Those leaders who are willing to admit to the limitations of their own styles are better able to draw from the different strengths of other people.

But you can't draw from someone's strengths if you don't see them.

We highly recommend that you learn to adapt to *all* TILT styles if you want your team to become high performing. The first step in doing this is realizing that your judgments about another person's work style interfere with your ability to collaborate. Make a habit of exploring points of view through the lens of other TILT styles. If you're willing to put forth the effort to do this, your communication style will begin to reflect what's important to others. When your communication improves, your ability to collaborate does, too.

Are you willing to shift your thinking and communication to support greater collaboration?

To make this shift, start by considering how other TILT styles see things differently than you. By becoming aware of the limitations of your own natural work style and broadening your perspective, you will:

1. Become *much* better at achieving your own goals by "TILT-ing" toward strengths you don't naturally exhibit (and never knew you had).
2. Ask questions that will help you relate to people who TILT differently, a powerful step to collaborating.

Here are some suggested questions to ask yourself to stretch you outside of your natural TILT style, particularly when you "over-TILT" toward your preferred strengths.

- **If you over-TILT toward impact, you might ask yourself**: Are we moving too quickly? What else do I need to consider? Have I thought through all the details here?

- **If you over-TILT toward connection, you might ask yourself**: Do I know specifically what we are going to do? Have we documented a plan? What are the tough conversations I need to have?

- **If you over-TILT toward clarity, you might ask yourself**: Are we too lost in the details right now? Do we have a clear vision of what success would look like? What does "good enough" look like?

- **If you over-TILT toward structure, you might ask yourself**: Have we considered how people will feel if we follow this process? Are we considering other people's perspectives or controlling things too much?

By asking yourself these questions, you start to think more like a person who naturally TILTS toward another style. How you think and how you communicate will adapt.

KNOW HOW TO ADAPT TO DIFFERENT SITUATIONS

If you want to improve your team's performance, it's up to you to shift your own style to match that of others. When individuals have the self-awareness to adapt to someone else's preferred style, they become excellent collaborators. When an entire *team* practices this together, it makes them agile.

Adapting your work style is not a one-time thing; it's something you do with everyone you work with. Start by observing patterns in the way your colleagues communicate and work. As their preferred work styles become apparent to you, you'll find yourself making requests that draw on people's strengths, using language that appeals to them. You begin to understand what's important to them and why they think so differently from you, and you see value in their perspective. You become highly proficient at dividing tasks and assigning accountability based on what each person is good at, and you know how to gain buy-in, simply by knowing how to ask.

The more you think through the lens of the four TILT styles, the more you'll discover ways to adapt your style to accommodate others.

For example, we once worked with a communications director struggling in his relationship with his executive boss. His boss was a fast-moving, impact-oriented type who wanted to make quick decisions and hated meetings that lasted longer than a half hour. The communications director was intimidated: whenever he met with his boss, she grew impatient and seemed disinterested in what he had to say.

As it turned out, the communications director had a natural clarity orientation. He walked into his boss's office with twenty slide decks packed with details. After learning about the TILT model, he realized he had to change his approach. Before the next meeting with his boss, he turned what would have been twenty slides into three. He later reported that the fifteen-minute meeting with his boss was one of the best he'd ever had. From that point forward, he modified his own style and, as a result, completely changed his working relationship with his boss.

Another manager we worked with had been struggling with a direct report. She gave him clear goals and instructions, but something was off. He didn't always follow her instructions, and she told us, "Sometimes I get the sense he doesn't trust me, but I don't know why." When we looked at her TILT profile, we saw she was naturally structure-oriented. She was great with instructions and process, but sometimes neglected how people felt.

Often, building trust is an exercise in "TILT-ing" toward connection. We asked the manager, "What would it look like to TILT toward connection to build trust?" Her first thought was to do a feedback listening tour to gain some insight into her employee's experience and build connection. After the meeting, she came back and said, "I was completely missing his Fundamental Why. He TILTs toward connection. I usually skip over the people part, which is the part he loves. I saw a different way for us to collaborate. Instead of expecting him to just follow my plan, I can include him in the planning process, working together with me in connection. He was excited about that idea."

While this kind of adaptation requires an ongoing effort to learn your colleague's style and preferences, it's helpful to have some general guidelines to adjust your communication for each TILT strength. These guidelines provide a starting point for adapting your communication to fit the TILT styles of the different people you work with:

- **Impact**: Be brief. Explain the big picture and Fundamental Why. Inspire with a description of the end result. They'll want to know: "Why is this important?"

- **Connection**: Check in, ask how they're doing. Include them and their ideas. Show you care. They'll want to know: "How will this affect others?"

- **Clarity**: Refer to facts/research. Provide details. Give planning time. Ask their opinion. They'll want to know: "What have we not considered?"

- **Structure**: Organize your ideas and thinking. Communicate the plan. Be specific. They'll want to know: "How will we do it?"

CREATE TEAM AGILITY

While the individuals on a team are responsible for adapting their own style to work better with others, teams as a whole can use the TILT to boost **team agility**—the ability to draw on their strengths and compensate for their weaknesses. Generally, a team tends to TILT toward one style or another, because the individuals on the team TILT in a particular direction.

We find that when teams are made up of people with shared TILT work styles, they often find it easy to work with each other. However, the team usually lacks the strengths of the other TILT styles not represented.

For instance, an engineering team we worked with was made up of some of the strongest developers in the state. Their meetings were dense with detail and highly structured. They were extremely skilled at solving technical problems. But something wasn't working. They were slow to produce results and got so lost in details they were working eighty hours a week without reaching their goals. Deadlines were missed; projects were delayed. Executives in the company consistently lauded the team's technical skills but admitted they often didn't know what the team was doing. While the team did well following instructions, they did not always think about the big picture and could not adapt when circumstances changed.

Using the TILT model, we asked the team to map out their primary TILT strengths directly onto the four quadrants. Each team member placed a dot and their name in the quadrant correlated with their primary TILT strength. As expected, the map showed a team filled with clarity- and structure-oriented TILTs. Not a single team member had their name in either the connection or the impact quadrant.

This provided some key information. While the team was great with the details and executing the plan (even practicing weekly project huddles), they often lacked the big-picture thinking an impact-oriented team typically exhibits. The executives didn't know what they were working on because the engineers neglected the connection-oriented skill of socializing their work and communicating with the executives. With such a heavy emphasis on the detail and structure associated with their preferred TILT styles, the engineers fell into the trap of slow decision-making and perfectionism. All in all, they'd lost sight of the vision, a common pitfall of teams without impact- and connection-oriented team members.

By mapping their TILTs like this, the team now had a visual display of their strengths and weaknesses. Somehow these gaps needed to be filled. They had to ask themselves, "How can each of us TILT more toward connection and impact? What can we each do to make sure we're socializing our work through the organization? What can we each do to ensure we don't lose sight of the big picture and get stuck in the weeds?"

We then asked them to consider who outside their team could support them in their effort to TILT more toward impact and connection. They identified an individual in the marketing/communications department whom they felt could socialize their work inside the organization and create more impact-style presentations for the executive team. They also scheduled a "vision" check-in once a month with their department director to ensure their projects still supported the organization's big picture vision.

With these additional supports in place, the team addressed their weaknesses and began moving quickly toward their goals. They also improved their ability to work cross-functionally, increasing partnership and visibility inside the marketing/communications and executive teams. Using the TILT model, the team could compensate for the strengths they didn't have, and everyone agreed the team had become significantly more agile.

To put the TILT model into practice like this, map out each team member on the TILT quadrants as in the previous example. Place each team member's name inside the appropriate quadrant. (Even if you haven't completed the TILT assessment, you can take an educated guess based on the information in this chapter.)

Then, looking at the map, ask yourselves:

☐ "What strengths do we naturally TILT toward?"
☐ "What strengths do we lack?"
☐ "What do we each need to do to compensate for the TILT strengths we lack?"
☐ "Who else in the organization can we partner with cross-functionally to make sure we make up for what we lack?"

One final note on the TILT and adapting your work styles: be aware that every individual on your team and in your company has personal strengths independent of their TILT preferences. These are built on personal history, influential relationships, and natural abilities. The more you can bridge differences, the easier it is to draw from others' strengths to build camaraderie and collaboration. Focusing on your team's strengths builds more strength!

PRACTICE FIVE

ADAPT YOUR WORK STYLE

STRUCTURE FOR APPLICATION

1. Map every person on your team on the TILT quadrant model. Together ask, "Where are we strong? Where do we need to build strength as a team?"

2. Any time you have a communications breakdown with someone, ask, "What is their preferred communication style on the TILT map? How can I adapt my style to fit theirs?"

3. As a team, determine what TILT strengths you'll need each time you start a project. Ask, "Is there anyone else in the organization we should partner with to make sure we are operating with all four strengths?"

4. Identify the strengths of each person on your team (including your manager). Write them out, and then share what you wrote in a one-on-one conversation. Ask your teammate what they perceive their own strengths to be and how they developed these based on their past experiences. Practice deep listening.

SIX

GET FOCUSED

"Time—the one asset none of us is ever going to get more of."
—GARY VAYNERCHUK, Chairman of VaynerX

Management consultancy McKinsey asked nearly 1,500 executives across the globe how they spent their time. Only 9 percent of the respondents said they were "very satisfied" with their current allocation of that precious resource. One-third of the respondents were "actively dissatisfied." Almost half did not think they were focusing on strategic priorities that guided the direction of the company.[50]

A lack of strategic focus and inadequate time management typically plague lower-performing teams. When an executive team lacks focus, so does the organization. Employees say things like, "We don't get enough information about the company's direction. Where are we going? Why are we working on what we're working on?"

We see this lack of focus on teams at all levels in many companies. Usually, they know they have a problem, but don't know what to do about it. People are busier than ever, but outcomes are scattered and misdirected. Meetings often produce *more* meetings. Projects are seriously overdue. Many projects have mysteriously disappeared.

High-performing teams, on the other hand, do less, but accomplish more. They focus on a few things and do them well. They have fewer meetings and make every meeting count. They spend most of their time on activities that produce the most results. They make clear decisions and commit to taking responsibility for executing them.

The practice of Getting Focused requires structure and discipline. It means being willing to say what you *will* work on, and what you will *not*. It's like "tightening the belt" on your time, which begins with how you *think* about your time.

80/20 YOUR PRIORITIES

In his book *The 80/20 Manager*, Richard Koch advises managers to apply the 80/20 principle in all decision-making. Also known as the Pareto Principle, the premise is that 80 percent of the results you get come from 20 percent of your input. And 80 percent of *those* results come from 20 percent of *that* input.[51]

Following Koch's advice, individuals focus primarily on activities that generate the highest output. At its core, the 80/20 principle says do less, accomplish more. In other words, the teams (and individuals) who produce the most results do not necessarily do the most work.

While you may have heard of the 80/20 principle and understand it conceptually, applying this rule can be challenging at first. It's not always a natural practice to focus your efforts on *only* what you're going to do. Most of us value hard work. We value saying "yes." Doing less takes a willingness to say "no" to what you are unwilling to work on. At first, for many managers, it feels as though they are "doing something wrong" when they do less.

But working *more* does not always yield the highest output. In fact, "too much to do" often means not enough gets done well. High-performance teams learn how to work *smarter* versus *more*, mainly focusing on **80/20 actions**. These are the actions or priorities that, if you focus on them, will bring about the greatest gains.

A process payments company we worked with decided that, in an oversaturated market, they would be the best in the world at *one* thing: processing payments for attorneys. While other payment solutions focused on many verticals, our client kept their focus narrow and dominated their one vertical of payments for attorneys. This meant saying no to a lot of other business opportunities outside of this vertical.

The company built a strong company culture and took good care of their people and, as a result, their people took exceptional care of their customers. Over time, the company moved into other verticals, but only after they had dominated their specific niche. Their focused strategy, seamless execution, and commitment to their people were the reason they made the Inc. 5000 fastest-growing companies in the US for nine consecutive years.

In his book *The 7 Habits of Highly Effective People*, Steven Covey uses the term "Rock" to describe a top priority. He recommends choosing only a few Rocks each year, because if everything is important, nothing is important.[52]

Rocks are examples of the 80/20 principle: focus on doing a few things well. The same concept can (and should) be applied to teams.

To put the 80/20 principle into practice, high-performing teams generally have three big, clear Rocks. Each team member should also have clearly defined individual Rocks to support the teams' top priorities. This is where 80 percent of your effort should go, because these hand-picked Rocks are the 20 percent of your input that will effect significant growth.

We coached one data-tech company that was working hard but had lost their focus. Demand for their service had increased, but they couldn't find enough data scientists to meet the demand. They struggled to convince talent to join them instead of Google and Facebook. Without the ability to grow internal capacity, they couldn't make the jump to the next level of their scale. They were doing a lot, but weren't growing.

We challenged this company to simplify and figure out what specific course of action would yield the growth they were looking for. We narrowed their focus to one big thing: instead of trying to be *like* their competitors, we recommended they differentiate themselves to create a unique market edge and attract top talent. They decided to become a company where young recruits could come and have the best possible career development experience they could get anywhere. The company developed an incredible training program to make that a reality. As the idea took off, they gained a unique reputation in their industry and talent started joining them instead of the large multinationals.

Here's what they did:

1. Defined and cascaded their Core Purpose (Fundamental Why) across the company
2. Created an annual goal of six new major clients to address customer concentration risks

3. Defined a ninety-day goal to launch a college recruiting and robust data scientist training program
4. Created an onshore location in the same time zone to offer consulting at one-third of the cost
5. Focused new employee onboarding around core purpose

This five-step strategy resulted in fast growth. The company no longer looked like other organizations; rather, they stood out. They secured new clients because the sales team focused on a targeted set of clients. Recruits were inspired to join the company because they saw the growth opportunity. The company's college recruiting effort was a huge success, and their near-shore office quickly boosted their competitive edge. Within a few years, they sold for an above-industry multiple-of-revenue (with no earn-out, recurring revenue, or long-term contracts). They excelled in the long run by doing less and creating a simpler, more focused strategy.

In his book, *Getting Results the Agile Way*, author J.D. Meier recommends the "Rule of 3."[53] This concept comes from software development techniques learned at Microsoft to increase team and personal focus. In keeping with the 80/20 principle, it suggests that you can usually focus on only three things at a time. Any more becomes too distracting to achieve well. With this in mind, there are not simply big, annual Rocks, but three quarterly priorities, three weekly priorities, and three daily priorities.

We suggest that teams and individuals on each team practice the Rule of 3. Start each year by identifying team Rocks and individual Rocks. Let these Rocks inform the team's (and team members') three quarterly goals, their three weekly goals, and their three daily goals. Eighty percent of the team's time should be spent on these **Big 3 Goals**.

Each team should ask:

☐ "What are our Big 3 Rocks for the year?"
☐ "What are our Big 3 Focus Goals this quarter?"
☐ "What are our Big 3 Focus Goals this week?"

Each individual should ask:

☐ "What are my Big 3 Rocks for the year?"
☐ "What are my Big 3 Focus Goals this quarter?"
☐ "What are my Big 3 Focus Goals this week?"
☐ "What are my Big 3 Focus Goals today?"

When actions do not fall under these Big 3, consider removing them from the team's to-do list. If they aren't a Big 3, but are still essential, ensure that the minimum required effort is spent on them.

The following page shows an easy way to rank your priorities so you can choose your 80/20 actions. Plot points on the grid below for each item on your to-do list, both yours and your team's. The lowest-input, highest-output activities should become the week's focus.

As you plot these points, you'll find you have tasks that are high input, low output. Give these tasks the lowest priority—they might need to be a "no" for the week. Ideally, you can also identify actions to remove from your to-do list completely. *This is a good thing.* Removing extra work from your team allows you and your teammates to focus on the higher-output actions. Just because something feels important doesn't mean it is.

These are the three buckets to use when assigning priority to high-input, low-output tasks: *delete, delegate,* and *delay.*

DECISION-MAKING GAUGE

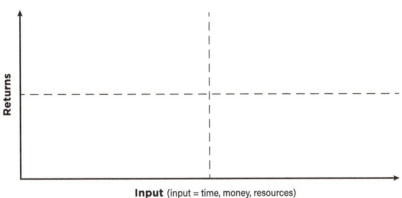

Input (input = time, money, resources)

Delete: When viewed objectively, these actions no longer need to be done. Cross them off the list.

Delegate: Is there someone else who can take this on? One manager we worked with felt guilty about asking others to do more work. However, using the "high-input/low-output grid," she saw she was putting too much upon herself. When she began delegating tasks, not only were others on her team happy to do them; they expressed gratitude for being trusted with additional responsibility. Over time, they took on far more than she had previously believed they could (or would). She realized she had failed to utilize her team's talent just because *she* felt bad. However, skillful delegation is a fundamental part of strong leadership.

Delay: Many teams complain that "everything has to be done yesterday." They miss deadlines and fail to complete projects because new priorities usurp current ones almost daily. But everything *doesn't* need to be done right away. With some objective discernment, you can choose what needs to be done now and what can wait.

One manager we worked with wanted to make sure the executive team was aware her team was important to the organization. She created an Excel spreadsheet for her employees to review all the projects the team was working on. She asked each team member to add anything they were working on to the list. The number of spreadsheet pages began to go up.

While it appeared the team was accomplishing a lot, they were actually scattered and lacking direction. They were doing so much they were having a hard time getting anything done. In his book *The 80/20 Principle*, Richard Koch explains our cleint's challenge like this: "Few people take objectives really seriously. They put average effort into too many things, rather than superior thought and effort into a few important things. People who achieve the most are selective as well as determined."[54]

We asked the team manager to apply the 80/20 actions grid to her spreadsheets. It took a while, and it required honesty about what produced the best outcomes. But using this tool, we helped the manager tighten up the team's priorities. Quickly, their meetings became focused on aligned goals. Team members worked on fewer goals, and projects started moving over the finish line. The quality of the team's work improved. While cutting out so much from the to-do list initially made them nervous, by the end of the year, they marveled at how many of their personal and team Rocks had been accomplished.

80/20 YOUR MEETINGS

While getting clear on your 80/20 priorities is key, how you focus your attention on accomplishing these priorities requires a different kind of focus: better meetings. This means having more focused meetings to address the (now-reduced) number of priorities you've agreed upon. It also means having fewer meetings.

Many people we work with feel like they're in meetings all day. When we ask a room filled with directors and managers how many of these meetings are a 10 on a scale of 1 to 10 (10 being great), most (if not all) say, "None of them." They tell us that meetings burn them out. Their meetings are long, people talk a lot, there's always a lot of work to do, and nothing seems to get accomplished.

Lower-performing teams have become so accustomed to meetings that feel dull, scattered, tense, and unproductive, they assume that's the way it must be. They accept it as "part of the job" to sit through them.

High-performing teams have fewer meetings with greater focus. These meetings are intentionally scheduled on the calendar rather than just calling a meeting for the sake of a meeting. Only those who need to attend have the meeting on the calendar. The team's focused meetings produce results quickly because conversations are highly structured. Instead of talking about everything at once, shifting from topic to topic, participants practice the discipline of focus throughout. In the rest of this chapter, we'll show you exactly how to do this.

Start by using the 80/20 principle to ask, "What do we really *need* to meet about this week?" Schedule meetings that serve your highest priorities. Eliminate, shorten, or delay meetings that may distract from these. What if you could cut out 10 percent of your meetings? 20 percent? How about 30 percent? What if fewer meetings meant better work? Would you rather have more meetings or more productivity?

Before scheduling a meeting, ask:

☐ "Does this meeting have a clear Fundamental Why?"

If the answer is "yes," then identify it.

If there is no clear Fundamental Why, then nothing is at stake. The meeting won't propel your team toward your goals. If the answer to "Why are we having this meeting?" doesn't serve the team's priorities, cancel it. If it does, identify the meeting's Fundamental Why in your meeting invite, so everyone can be prepared to participate fully around a focused topic.

80/20 YOUR CALENDAR

Individuals on high-performing teams take full responsibility for their calendars, and we always encourage individuals on teams to "80/20" their calendars. This means saying "no" when necessary, especially to meetings you don't need to attend. This can be a stretch for some, so start small. Can you reduce your meetings by 10 percent by asking:

☐ "Does this meeting have a Fundamental Why?"
☐ "Do I need to be there?"

When the answer is "no," cut it from your schedule. High-performing teams offer team members the prerogative to say "no" if declining a meeting invitation creates space to do less and accomplish more. Remember, if you are a team's manager, you must model the ability to say "no." If *you* aren't willing to say "no"—or accept a "no" from individuals on your team—your team won't say "no," either. Set the expectation that you trust your team to say "no" to meetings when they don't need to be there.

We worked with one director who was recently promoted to his position. He was shocked by the number of meetings he now had to attend. When he looked at his calendar, he said that some weeks he had entire days full of back-to-back meetings. "I don't have time to get any actual work done," he told us.

This issue is common. We asked him first if it was necessary to be at every one of those meetings. Using the 80/20 grid, he mapped out the priority levels of each meeting and said, "Absolutely not." But when we suggested he decline the meetings he didn't need to attend, he looked shocked. "You're saying I should just say 'no'? I can't do that." He was concerned that saying "no" would cause resentment among his colleagues.

But eventually, he agreed to eliminate 5 percent of his meetings by declining to attend when a meeting didn't have a clear Fundamental Why. At first, he was nervous about it. But after a month, he realized it was okay to sit a few meetings out. In three months, the number grew to 20 percent declines, which freed up a significant amount of time on his calendar. He also discovered he really *didn't* have to be there. If he needed to know what happened at a particular meeting, he would request the notes. He had more time to work, and his teammates accommodated him by streamlining their information, so he got what he needed.

He could do this because his team was working together to adopt all seven high-performance principles. When everyone understands the importance of a Fundamental Why, for instance, and why you should 80/20 your calendar, they won't question a director's decision to decline a meeting. And it will create permission for others to say no when there is a valid reason to sit something out.

If you are the one organizing a meeting, don't invite everyone on the team every time. Meetings are costly if you add up the hourly wage of everyone attending. If you find it hard to leave someone off, make their attendance optional. They will probably thank you. If they need to be "in the know," email them the notes you create in the meeting (see below). Make the 80/20 decision for them.

HAVE GREAT MEETINGS

By calling a meeting, you're deciding that a meeting is the most important use of your time. The Fundamental Why should be so clear that everyone invited knows they should be there (and why). The meeting needs to have something at stake—what happens in that meeting will drive the team toward their goals as much as anything else they could do. As Pat Lencioni says in his book *The Motive*, "Meetings should be exhausting, intense, and a little anxious because if there's anything at stake—the livelihood of employees and vendors, the success of the customer—it's something worth talking about in meetings."[55]

Lower-performing meetings typically fall short of this aspiration. Usually, the meeting has been called because that's just what you're supposed to do when something comes up: call a meeting. Lower-performing meetings do not advance the action. The conversations get derailed and go down **rabbit holes**. People in the meetings appear distracted, checking their phones or email.

It often comes as a surprise when we recommend that every single meeting should be great. People think we're setting the bar high, or even being sarcastic! They're so used to average meetings; they don't even *consider* planning a "great" meeting.

But it *is* possible to have great meetings—all the time. First, the Fundamental Why of the meeting must be so compelling that everyone *expects* the meeting to be great. To have great meetings, here are some basic ground rules to consider:

1. Every participating team member must attend the meeting ready to participate fully.
2. Start and end the meeting on time, every time.
3. Practice deep listening when others are talking.
4. Have a note taker.
5. No outside work or communication should occur while in the meeting. (This means no phones.)
6. Take breaks if necessary.
7. Everyone participates and leaves with a clear understanding of what they need to do.

FOLLOW A CLEAR MEETING STRUCTURE

There are many kinds of meetings a team might have:

- A daily huddle designed for fast information flow to identify obstacles
- A weekly strategic or project meeting designed to solve problems collectively
- A monthly meeting designed to solve more complex problems
- A quarterly two-day strategic planning offsite

Every meeting should have a clear, focused structure. Here, we'll focus on the building blocks of the weekly team or project meeting. From our experience, weekly meetings are the most common, most misunderstood, and most poorly executed corporate meetings. The building blocks of this structure can be adapted for other types of meetings as well. But we recommend all weekly and project meetings follow this basic structure:

1. **Checking in**: What is on each person's mind?
2. **Fundamental Why**: Why is this meeting important?
3. **Agenda**: What will we discuss?
4. **Parking lot**: What do we need to discuss at a later date?
5. **Decision registry**: What decisions have been made? Who will do what by when?
6. **Quick feedback**: How was this meeting?
7. **Follow-up email**

1. Checking In

Checking in is a straightforward way to increase focus in a meeting. When you sit down to dinner with a friend, you Don't start talking about your problems until you spend time finding out how your friend is doing. Many unfocused meetings start with people doing what they wouldn't do to a friend: showing up in a room and immediately talking about all the problems they need to address. Everyone at the meeting has a lot going on—personally and professionally—and it can be difficult to turn that stuff off. By checking in with each other first, you support a smoother transition to more in-depth subject matter.

Checking in doesn't need to be a big deal, just a short time at the beginning of each meeting to give everyone a chance to speak. Very simply, you're connecting with each other by answering a personal question like:

☐ "How are you doing today?"
  Or
☐ "What's on your mind?"

For longer meetings with fewer people, each person takes about a minute to do this. At shorter meetings, you can limit the responses to a one-phrase answer (e.g., "doing great," "a little distracted," "tired," "excited to be here," etc.).

The check in is an opportunity for each person to settle in and transition from whatever they were doing before the meeting.

2. Fundamental Why

This one is easy. After everyone has had a chance to check in, the organizer of the meeting states the Fundamental Why (i.e., Why, exactly are we having this meeting?) and asks, "Does anyone have anything to add?"

3. Agenda

The meeting organizer reviews the proposed agenda and again asks, "Does anyone have anything to add?" Each item on the agenda should clearly support the team's priorities. If you add up the amount of time and number of people who are in meetings you will see that they are very expensive. To get an effective return on a meeting, the agenda should be 75 percent problem solving or learning and only 25 percent reporting. The agenda should zero in on problems the team can collectively solve.

As you progress the agenda, stick to one item at a time. Each agenda item is a different conversation. The context of each is different. If you are talking about a response you need to provide to an internal stakeholder, you need to have a different kind of conversation than you would if you were discussing your next hire. What and how you think shifts for each agenda topic. That's why it's important to stay on ONE agenda topic at a time.

When conversations bleed together, the context gets confusing. People say, "Wait, what are we talking about here?" and decisions are harder to make. The group keeps going down rabbit holes and veering off topic. A 2020 survey of 757 workers conducted by meeting optimization company Clockwise found that off-topic conversations were the number one meeting challenge people faced.[56] Teams go down rabbit holes because there's so much to talk about. Something reminds someone of another issue the team needs to address, and the team starts talking about *that*. High-performing teams maintain a commitment to the subject at hand until decisions are made. To do this requires discipline, but it works.

4. Parking Lot

One effective way to prevent rabbit holes is to use the **parking lot**. The parking lot is a record of off-topic issues that arise in a meeting. Anytime something comes up unrelated to the meeting's purpose, ask quickly:

☐ "Does this need to go to the parking lot?"

The answer is "yes" if it's an issue the team doesn't need to talk about right now. If so, put it in the parking lot to incorporate into a later meeting. *Don't let rabbit holes lure you away from your focus.* Stay disciplined about this. Write the topic down and steer the conversation back to the agenda. Before scheduling the next meeting, look at your parking lot and rank the priorities. Which of your parking lot items can be taken offline or handled one-on-one? Which issues need to be discussed in a future meeting?

We worked with one executive team whose visionary CEO had new ideas every time the team got together. One topic would inspire the CEO to suddenly think of a new idea, and the discussion would shift toward his new idea. The rest of the team had a hard time keeping up. Decisions often weren't made, and the team's to-do list got longer. Not only did the executive team have too much to do, but the organization as a whole did, too.

These constant rabbit holes were disruptive, and the team let us know. We suggested they implement the parking lot technique. Every time the team met as a group, a different person took responsibility for managing the parking lot (including the CEO). Any time the meeting went down a rabbit hole, the person in charge of the parking lot wrote the topic down and brought the team back into focus.

At first, the discipline brought up a lot of resistance. Running meetings this way felt confining to the team. But, since every person had the chance to run the parking lot, they all began to see how often the team got distracted. They adopted a collective commitment to stay on topic, and their meetings improved in both focus and performance. Eventually, what felt uncomfortable and restrictive at first, became a key team practice that made their meetings (and their organization) better.

5. Decision Registry

Ideally, you decide on every agenda item on the list. As you complete each agenda item, record your decisions in a **decision registry**. If no decision gets made, move the topic to another meeting. All decisions should be documented and agreed upon. This prevents people from leaving the meeting not knowing if a decision was made or just talked about, and it forces people to document exactly what decision was made.

By answering these questions during the meeting, you ensure that a decision is made:

1. "Do we need to take action on this?"
2. "If yes, what outcome do we want?"
3. "What are some options to get there?"
4. "Which of these options will we try?"
5. "What, exactly, will we do?"
6. "If action is required, who does what by when?"

Never leave a meeting with ambiguity about decisions. If numbers 5 and 6 do not have a clear answer, you likely haven't come to a decision. Unfortunately, this happens in almost every lower-performing team meeting we've observed, leading to squandered resources and less-than-desirable outcomes. Sometimes, it's easier to talk about something endlessly than to make a decision. High-performance teams make decisions, even the tough ones.

All decisions and all answers to number 6 (who does what by when) must be written down by the note taker.

6. Quick Feedback

At the end of the meeting, have participants rank the meeting from 1 to 10 and ask for solution-oriented feedback (i.e., what worked about the meeting and what could we do better next time?). Use what you learn to make the next meeting better.

7. Follow-up Email

After the meeting, the combined decision registry is shared via email with the team. It notes all decisions made in the meeting, and who will do what by when. Share the email with all meeting participants as well as those who were not there but need to know.

PRACTICE SIX

GET FOCUSED

STRUCTURE FOR APPLICATION

1. Embrace the 80/20 principle, so that you're achieving more by doing less. Remember, 80 percent of your results should come from 20 percent of your input.

2. Get clear on team and individual Big 3 Focus Goals (i.e., your Rocks) for the year, quarter, and week. Make sure daily priorities work toward those Big 3 Focus Goals.

3. Practice 80/20 meeting scheduling. Ask: Do we need this meeting, or can this be done one-on-one or even through email?

4. Make sure every meeting has a clear, written Fundamental Why and Agenda beforehand. If it doesn't, cancel the meeting.

5. Start every meeting allowing everyone to check in about how they're doing.

6. To avoid going down rabbit holes, list any off-topic issue in your parking lot. Have a different person in each meeting manage the parking lot.

7. Make clear decisions about every agenda item, including who does what by when.

8. Write out your decision registry. Share it with everyone in the meeting and those who need to know.

SEVEN
GET IT DONE

*"A dream is just a dream. A goal is a dream
with a plan and a deadline."*
—HARVEY MACKAY, author of
Swim with the Sharks Without Being Eaten Alive

You probably have highly skilled people on your team with great intentions and ideas. And still, things don't get done. Projects start strong, then for whatever reason, they stall. Perhaps a new initiative takes resources away from the current one, or a director in another department calls the whole thing off. Maybe people don't know how to ask for the resources they need. In many cases, individuals simply aren't doing what they said they would do. We frequently hear frustrated managers say, "I wish people would just Get It Done," but nothing happens.

Why?

Many people don't know *how* to get things done. They don't know how to identify key stakeholders or decision-makers. They don't write out plans that include who will do what by when. They may not even remember *why* they're working on what they're working on. Sometimes, top-level decisions render a project obsolete—but nobody remembers to tell the team. (You might be surprised at how true all of these are in *your* organization.)

We first identified this issue after a few years of working with one of our flagship clients. They had already implemented the key practices of the Fundamental Why, deep listening, strengths, solutions-oriented feedback, and getting focused. They were breaking records in growth and revenue.

But the CEO said something was still missing.

According to the CEO, if an executive team member wasn't actively working on a project, he doubted it would ever get done. He knew next-level managers were working hard, but wasn't always sure *what* they were doing. Even simple decisions—like making a change in the break room—would find their way back to him.

He said he could "count on one hand" the staff members he trusted to consistently get things done. He named each of them and said, "Can you teach *everyone* to be more like that? We need more people to step up and own *results*, not just the tasks they're assigned."

This CEO wanted to create a culture of ownership, where people internalized responsibility—and personal gratification—for getting a job done well. He wanted his team to take it upon themselves to see projects to completion and care deeply about achieving the best possible outcomes.

To reach this goal, we introduced the elements of this seventh practice—Get It Done—into the day-to-day framework of the client organization. A year later, the company experienced their first year of exponential growth.

Teams that accelerate are teams where every member owns the success of the whole team. Managers can't make this choice on their own. Great communication, leadership, and culture-building don't matter unless everyone on the team takes on accountability and chooses to own the results they are responsible for.

As a team (and company), you must commit to bringing tasks "over the finish line," a discipline that requires concrete action plans and doing what you say you'll do. When teams do this well, it's like a crew team rowing in unison. Done poorly, it's like a cup of marbles spilling onto the floor.

Teams aren't the only ones who need plans of action; individual contributors do, too. We often hear managers complain that their direct reports have a lot of projects in the works, but many of these projects fizzle over time. They also report that new initiatives get greeted with excitement, but when enthusiasm wanes, so does the follow-through. One manager we worked with summed it up well, "My team is passionate, and they work hard, but we start a whole lot more than we finish."

Practice 6, Get Focused, is crucial for prioritizing tasks and making sure your team is only working on essential projects. Once that focus is in place, this seventh practice will guarantee that you finish what you start by having a concrete action plan in place. This chapter outlines the key pieces of an effective plan, which includes assigning accountability for each task. This practice is so important, we recommend never starting any new work until a plan has been written out to ensure success. And everyone on the team needs to commit to planning and follow-through like this, not just the project manager.

WRITE OUT YOUR PLANS BEFORE
MOVING INTO ACTION

As a manager, it's your job to identify key decision-makers, assign resources, and remove roadblocks for each project, campaign, or line of business. In other words, you're managing a lot of moving parts. While you might think you don't have time to write out a detailed plan, the discipline to do so saves you time and increases the probability that everybody will follow through—without undue intervention by you.

If a plan hasn't been written out, there is no plan. Instead, there has been a conversation about a plan, including each person's memory of what was said. When you write out a plan, you have a **visual display** that everybody can refer to throughout the life cycle of a project or task.

High-performing teams practice the discipline of writing out detailed plans *before* moving into action. As a result, your team will be more intentional about their work, and you will avoid wasted effort on tasks that don't support your goal.

When we first begin working with executive teams who aren't yet in the habit of writing out detailed plans (and following them), they make a lot of decisions on the fly. Project trajectories get sidetracked, especially when the volume of activity is high. People barely remember what they agreed upon a week ago. They end up wasting time on less important tasks and not spending enough time working toward personal, team, and company goals.

Usually, after just one strategic planning session with us, a lower-performing team experiences a rapid turnaround. By applying the 80/20 principle, they get clear on their focused actions and write out a plan for each. Often, we see this result in tangible revenue growth over a period of three months or less.

In this chapter, we break down the key elements of **planning to get things done**, a skillset that should be taught and applied at every level of the company. While a rigorous planning routine might be necessary at the executive level, most teams and individuals only need to practice the five basic steps of planning, as outlined below. By keeping it simple, planning can be done any time you start a new initiative. Note: *Some forms of project and team planning require greater complexity than others. But the goal here is that everyone on your team and in your company understands the basics of effective planning to get things done in your organization. And it's not just the manager that needs to do this—set the expectation that your team members come to you having already done this work when taking on self-directed initiatives.*

The five steps of effective planning are:

1. Fundamental Why
2. Vision of Wild Success
3. Current State
4. Roadmap
5. Accountabilities + Stakeholders

Step 1: Fundamental Why—Why Does This Need to Happen?

Any new project or initiative plan should first answer the question, "Why does this need to happen?" The answer should be compelling enough to motivate the team to act. If the answer to this question does not move you toward your big priorities, take it off your list. Your team already has enough to do.

Be honest here. A lot of work you're doing now may not need to happen anymore. One team we worked with looked at their list of "to-dos" and did the work of answering the question, "Why are we doing this?" It was disheartening for them to take an honest look at what they'd been doing, sometimes for months. For much of the list, the only truthful answers to "Why" were "I don't know" or "because this is what we've always done."

The reason for identifying the Fundamental Why for each project may seem obvious, but most project teams unintentionally skip this step, even though they think they've done it.

We once worked with a top project manager on a mission-critical compliance project at a Fortune 100 company. We asked each team member on this PM's team to document the Fundamental Why of the project. The project manager got annoyed with us because "they had real work to do." Then, to the project manager's shock, the team members couldn't agree on why they were embarking on the project in the first place. They proceeded to articulate different starting points, and different destinations as well. When a team can't agree on why they are doing something, they'll have very different ideas about where they're going.

The Fundamental Why is like a preflight check that clarifies the reason to fly before takeoff. It saves time, conserves fuel, creates and maintains alignment, and enables teams to reach their destination—together.

Step 2: A Vision of Wild Success

Creating a vision of success focuses your attention on what you want. (We'll get to the "wild" part in a moment.) By writing out a clear, compelling vision of what success looks like, you help other people see it, too. When teams share a vision, they channel their unique talents to collaborate to bring the vision into reality.

A vision paints a picture of a bright future. In other words, you need to actually see something in your mind that hasn't happened yet, which is a natural part of human psychology. Everyone has imagined getting something they want at some point in their life. Creating a vision is a way of intentionally using this innate skill to achieve results.

Many executives are accustomed to painting big, bold visions to gain buy-in from their teams. But not always. One executive team we worked with in the financial sector loved learning about feedback and prioritization, but when it came to talking about vision, one of the members shared his skepticism.

"You lost me when you started talking about vision," he said. "That's too woo-woo for me."

But we pointed out that every team has a vision of what might happen in the future. On this team, they did talk a lot about the future—all the things they *didn't* want to see happen. They focused mostly on what could go wrong rather than right.

"We need to stop all these arguments; people need to complain less; we need to clear up all these logistical problems, etc." In fact, when we asked the team what it would actually *look like* if they got what they wanted, they had a hard time coming up with a shared vision. They kept returning to the problems they wished weren't problems anymore.

The team was so caught up in their negativity bias, all they talked about was what they didn't want. As you might expect, morale was low, and results were mediocre.

By getting clear on what your future as a company could look like, you'll generate insights about how to get there. You'll talk differently about where you're going. Great leaders describe the future they want, so others know where they are being led.

Here is an easy way to access the part of your psychology that brings a vision to life:

1. Close your eyes.
2. Imagine you're holding a lemon.
3. Imagine you are slowly slicing the lemon into quarters.
4. Imagine you take the lemon slice up to your mouth, and you bite into it.

As you imagined this, did you have an actual experience of tasting something sour? Maybe your mouth even watered a little.

You can use a similar approach to create a vision that excites you and everybody around you. If you're descriptive enough, you'll *literally* experience a response in your body. If you imagine something sad, you'll feel sad. If you imagine something happy, you'll feel happy. If you imagine a vision that inspires you, you'll feel inspired.

Now let's talk about a **vision of "wild" success**, starting with the past, the present, and the future.

The past is everything that has happened before this moment. From one second ago to thousands of years ago, everything that has already happened is in the past.

Then there's the present, the present moment, right now. You're reading this sentence right now, at this moment. Perhaps you're sitting in a chair. The past is behind you, the future is in front of you, but right now, you are present.

In this present moment, you can imagine a future outcome you want. You can imagine either a predictable future, or an unpredictable future.

> Here's where you ask yourself, "What does *wild* success look like for me?"
>
> Imagine what it looks like, feels like, and sounds like. Speak it out. Write it out. A vision of wild success describes an *unpredictable future*. It's unpredictable because it has never been done before. To create this kind of vision, you leave the past behind. Just because "it's always been like this" doesn't mean it needs to be that way in the future. *If your response isn't unpredictable, you'll get predictable results.*
>
> What would really excite you and your team? High-performing teams imagine—down to the finest detail—a future that looks *outrageously* better. They ask:
>
> ☐ "What does *wild* success look like for us?"
> ☐ "What would be *really* exciting to achieve?"
> ☐ "Are we thinking big enough?"

In his book *A Lapsed Anarchist's Approach to Building a Great Business*, visioning expert Ari Weinzweig says that the process of coming up with a compelling vision "truly does get people to actively go after the future of their choosing, instead of just trying to get away from what they don't like about the present...the process gives us the power to alter the entire way we work with the world around us."[57]

Unfortunately, many teams suffer from a vision that describes a predictable future. It's predictable because you're saying, "We know what status quo looks like, so we will shoot for that, or only slightly better." Lower-performing teams set goals and expectations for what's *likely* to occur based on past results. They keep their goals small or set them based on fixing what's wrong right now (i.e., what we *don't* want anymore versus what we *do* want). They plan for the likely scenario without expanding what could be possible if they dreamt big. And when unconventional ideas come up, they spend a lot of time discussing why they won't work. They expect predictable results and sometimes actually achieve less than that.

Wild success is not a likely or predictable future. It's unlikely and unpredictable because it's never been accomplished before. By setting your sight much higher, you can achieve what might seem impossible right now. If you *don't* aspire to the unlikely, your results will be predictable (and mediocre) at best. Things might turn out okay, but without a vision of wild, unpredictable success, you may never know how great you can be.

To break the habit of mediocrity, first articulate what greatness looks like.

> We recommend teams spend time brainstorming about their vision of wild success before starting every project. To do this, you will want to ask yourselves a series of questions:
>
> ☐ "What will the results of the project look like?"
> ☐ "What will people be doing and saying when we complete it?"
> ☐ "How will people have a better experience of our product or service? How will their lives be better?"

☐ "What impact will we have made on our company?
On our customers? On society?"

☐ "How will we know we've been wildly successful?"

Be sure to include the perspective of everyone on the project team. Combine everybody's ideas into a written statement that describes how you collectively envision wild success. Be specific, so everyone understands what you're trying to accomplish. In Cameron Herold's book *Double Double*, he describes this process as creating a "painted picture" of your vision, a practice that helped scale the wildly successful 1-800-Got-Junk.[58]

Step 3: The Current State: Where Are We Now?

Your vision creates a gap between where you are and where you want to be. To make your vision of the future happen, you first need to get very clear about where you are now. By doing this, you can make more educated, thoughtful decisions about the actions you need to take to close the gap.

Even though a high-performing team has a vision, they don't start *planning* until they have a big-picture perspective of the present. They ask the question:

"Where are we now?"

We recommend having a **10,000-foot conversation** to assess the big picture of your current state with input from all team members (like getting up to 10,000 feet to see the landscape below). This exercise will help you gain objectivity on the current strengths, obstacles, and potential of your project or goal.

The 10,000-foot conversation follows our strengths-based feedback approach, beginning with "what is going well." When you focus on what's going well first, people tend to adopt a less defensive posture, and you can compile a more accurate perspective. The truth is a lot is always going well, but you probably forget this because you spend so much time thinking about what's going wrong.

> To have this big-picture conversation, ask yourselves:
>
> ☐ "Considering the Fundamental Why of our project or initiative, *what is going well* right now?"
> ☐ "*What is in the way* for us right now that's making our vision hard to accomplish? What are the gaps we need to address?"

Write your responses in list form on a flip chart or shared document. Be sure to include *everyone's* perspective. At the end of the conversation, you should have a clear, documented picture of your current state. You'll have a better understanding of your team's strengths to build from as you start working toward your vision. You will also have identified your "in the ways" to resolve. Keep in mind that every team, project, and organization will have many "in the ways" to resolve. The work of great leadership is to continue moving toward your vision while effectively addressing everything that gets in your way.

Step 4: A Roadmap: How Will We Get There?

Former CEO of American Express Kenneth Chenault said, "Many people don't focus enough on execution. If you make a commitment to get something done, you need to follow through on that commitment."[59] Often, big ideas and exciting visions get dropped once the work starts. Without a clear plan in place, your vision is just a wish. Your roadmap closes the gap between your current state and your vision. Your roadmap answers the question, "How will we get there?"

Often, lower-performing teams try to achieve bigger and better results by doing the same things they've done in the past. Creating an effective roadmap requires choosing options you've never tried before, which is the *only* way to achieve a vision you've never achieved before.

Creating your roadmap requires having two different kinds of conversations:

1. An options conversation, i.e., What *could* we try?
2. An actions conversation, i.e., What are we *actually* going to do?

The first question ("What could we try?") is an **options conversation**. This is a conversation that explores all the different possible approaches to addressing what's in your way to move toward your vision.

As a team, ask yourselves, "What could we try to move toward our vision? How could we address what's currently in the way?" Always take actions that leverage your team's strengths when possible.

To energize this brainstorming session, we recommend an approach called **playing what ifs**.

When "playing what ifs," everyone on the team contributes. To begin, everyone spends a few moments reviewing the current state. Then, each person writes down suggestions for how to address what's currently in the way. After everyone has written down their ideas, each person shares. Instead of just reading it aloud, however, start each idea with "What if we...[and say the idea]." (i.e., What if we created a collective dashboard for our project status?)

Rather than arguing about whether or not an idea will work, write each idea on the flip chart or shared document. This is not a time to debate (you'll do that when you make decisions about what you *will* do). Rather, you want to get everybody's ideas out and let the juices flow. Ideally, ideas build upon each other. Don't move to question 2 until you have exhausted your list of ideas about what you *could* try.

Another easy (and fun) way to discuss options is **future-telling**. In this exercise, the team imagines their desired vision has already happened.

Imagine you are already in the future you envision. As a team you answer the question:

"How did we get here?"

Everyone takes turns recounting their steps as though the vision has already been realized. It's like you've arrived in the future, and you're telling the story of how you got there. All ideas get written down. No arguing or debating about what will work—and what won't. Usually, you'll start seeing options you've never considered, which will help inform the actions you ultimately take.

After you've created your list of options, it's time to move into the **actions conversation**. This is where you debate the options on your list and decide what to do. Answer the question:

"Looking at our options, what will we actually do and why?"

Apply the 80/20 principle. Choose the course of action you think will yield the best results. Break this down into tasks and you've got your roadmap.

Step 5: Accountabilities: Who Does What by When?

Your plan isn't complete until each task on your roadmap has ONE person's name next to it and a "by when." Now, remember, you made a list of *who does what by when* in Practice 6, Get Focused, while completing your decision registry. The list you make now can be an extension of that list, with more detail as you break down each step of what needs to get done.

Accountabilities (Who does what by when):

1. *What* needs to be done?
2. *Who* will do it?
3. *By when* will that person do it?

There must be a *single* name next to each action item, including a date for completion. Accountability always belongs to a single person, *not* a group of people. Additionally, if there's no date next to the name, it's not an actual accountability. It is just a "to-do" whenever. (This part *must* be written down, or, chances are, it will be forgotten.)

Oftentimes, a project can't be completed without support from outside the team. For this reason, also ask:

"Who else do we need to include and what do we need from them?"

EXECUTE YOUR PLAN WITH INTEGRITY

When accountabilities have been identified in writing, everybody can mobilize. But this mobilization will only yield results when a team is held together by one guiding principle—**integrity**.

What exactly *is* integrity? We have found the simplest, easiest-to-apply definition of this term in the book *The Primes* by Chris McGoff, who defines it as:[60]

Integrity = Say → Do

A lot has been said about integrity, but when it comes down to it, being a person of integrity means following through on your word. You either do what you say, or you don't. Just like your mindset, integrity is a choice.

Of course, there will always be times when something doesn't get done. But on a high-performing team, people don't spend a lot of time explaining *why* they didn't do what they said they would. Instead, team members own the break in integrity. They say, "I missed my deadline. I'm sorry. Here is what I will do." They don't spend a lot of time making excuses. They simply own the break and correct their course.

MAKE POWERFUL REQUESTS

Getting into action often involves making requests of people who aren't necessarily accountable for the project's success. For this reason, high-performing teams practice asking clear, actionable requests for support from non-accountable colleagues. Projects move forward quickly when you collaborate with integrity and make clear, powerful requests. We recommend using the five steps from your written plan to form your requests:

1. Share the Fundamental Why of the project or initiative.
2. Share the vision of success.
3. Describe the gap between the current state and where you want to go.

4. Articulate the specific help you believe you need from the person and how this will help your vision.

5. Ask if they can and *will* support you with this request and by when they will do it. Let them know you will add their name—and a date—to your accountability list.

SAMPLE PLAN TO GET THINGS DONE AND POWERFUL REQUESTS

Here is a sample plan that follows all five steps of intentional planning. It also includes an example of a powerful request to move the plan into action. Use this as a guide to help your team build the Get It Done practice.

Step 1: Fundamental Why

Elevate our team's ability to get things done with the intention of doubling our output in less time so we will have happier, more successful team members.

Step 2: Vision of Wild Success

[Speaking as if the future you want is your current reality.]

Vision: What does it look like when we double our output and get things done with integrity, accountability, and ownership?

We exceeded our targets by 3x last year and are on track for a record year now. We work together almost seamlessly. We spend most of our time moving toward a vision of what we want. We solve problems by looking at the big picture, making strategic decisions about what we will (and won't) do. We eliminated 25 percent of our meetings. One hundred percent of tasks that support our

vision will each have a single person's name holding the accountability for its success. We make requests that are clear, compelling,
and easy to fulfill. We do what we say, and make sure to own it if
we don't. We use 20 percent more vacation time. We've been fea-
tured in *Entrepreneur* magazine and are making more money than
ever. Our happy hours are legendary because we all love working
together so much.

Step 3: Current State

What's going well to support getting things done (your actual lists
will likely be longer):

- We're all passionate.
- We get along well for the most part.
- We do get some results now.
- Some projects get done.
- We're all highly skilled and respect each other's skill.
- We are high-performing in our individual roles.
- Company vision is inspiring.
- Our values are great.

What's in the way of our performance:

- Communication is not as good as it could be.
- We do a lot of work that probably doesn't need to be done
  anymore.
- Collaboration is not great across departments.
- We're overworked.
- High stress.

- Seems like we're always running and chasing the next best thing.
- Balls get dropped, and there are a lot of tasks stalled without progress.
- Sometimes we resist doing things differently.
- Our company culture is more shoot from the hip than long-term strategic.

Step 4: Roadmap

Options Conversation

Example:

"What if we..."

(Remember, not everything is going to be done from this list. These options just help you decide what to actually do.)

- Examined all of our current projects and figured out if the Fundamental Why still makes sense for us
- All read the chapter on Get It Done
- Had HR create a formal leadership training program internally
- Started implementing the five steps of intentional planning in our planning meetings
- Brought on a new project manager
- Worked with the executive team to help us have these practices shared across the company
- Spent a whole meeting just talking about our vision
- Got more specific on accountabilities in writing
- Turned intentional planning into a key success metric for each of us

- Could have complete integrity to do what we say, or communicate when we don't, 100 percent of the time

Actions Conversation + Accountabilities
(Who Will Do What by When)

What we will actually *do* to bring us closer to our vision of wild success:

1. Conduct a team audit of our current project list. Ensure we are clear on the Fundamental Why of each initiative. What can we get rid of?
    - Salina to schedule meeting by 1/17
    - Ruwan to deliver final report 2/03

2. Implement the five steps of intentional planning in our next project meeting. Vivek 2/1

3. At the end of every meeting, ensure that any actions we decide to take have a "who does what by when." Vivek (beginning with the next meeting on 2/1)

4. Set a goal for doing everything we say for five business days. At the end of the five days, come together and discuss what it would take to bring this discipline into our team. Raquel to schedule by 2/14

5. New visual dashboard for project tasks. Raquel by 3/15

Who else do we need to include in this?

1. Robert from IT. Request that he help us implement the visual dashboard to support. (Raquel will make request of Robert by 2/4.)

2. *Executive Sponsor*: Cindy, COO. Make sure she approves use of new software or has given that decision-making authority to Robert. (Salina will ensure Robert has decision-making authority from Cindy by 2/4.)

Example of a Powerful Request

Hi Robert,

Our team is taking on an initiative to double our output and significantly decrease the time we're currently spending on logistical issues. We think we can 3x our delivery in a year and need some IT support to help us do that. We want to upgrade our project management software to something that allows us all to look and work in it more easily, and we have identified the software to use.

Are you able to dedicate any of your staff to help us get the new project display software up and running? Our goal is that we have this implemented by 3/15. This would mean that all 6 VPs have been trained in the new PM software, are entering 100 percent of new projects in it as of 3/15, and use it weekly in their report-out meetings. Can you let me know by COB tomorrow by text or email if you can fulfill this request or if there is anything you need to make this happen?

Please let me know if you'd like more information or would like to discuss.

Thank you!

Raquel

PRACTICE SEVEN
GET IT DONE

STRUCTURE FOR APPLICATION

1. Articulate a clear Fundamental Why for any project or initiative.

2. Create a clear, compelling vision of wild success.

3. Document a collective point of view of your current state.

4. Have a conversation about options for potential actions.

5. Decide what you will do.

6. Write out a plan of accountability: who will do what by when.

7. Do what you say.

8. Make clear, powerful requests.

PUT IT INTO PRACTICE

"Ultimately leadership is about creating new realities."
—JOSEPH JAWORSKI, Founder of the
American Leadership Forum

Now you know the seven fundamental practices that will make you a better team by Friday. Did any of them surprise you? Do you already incorporate some of the practices, even if only partially? Take a moment to assess your team to figure out which of the seven practices you're missing and where you want to start. We recommend you start with Practice 1.

The results will extend far beyond what you can imagine from your vantage point now. If you've struggled to improve your team's performance only to find yourself dealing with the same issues month after month (or year after year), you'll be astonished by the changes you see. When teams apply these practices, people get fired up. They're excited about what they do and speak excitedly about their work with others. They choose to take ownership of their work and seek out ways to improve.

In other words, they *care*.

Because this type of deep, foundational transformation is a team effort, you may want to work through the book together. Spend one month on a single practice. Put that practice on every meeting agenda and work the exercises together in your meetings. Ask yourselves the questions included throughout the chapter. Ideally, every team member will also commit to practicing with each other outside of meetings. After you feel you have integrated one practice, move on to the next.

What will happen to your team over a short period of time will amaze you. Within the first week of applying the practices, productivity and engagement increase. Within a few weeks of incorporating these practices, we see previously disenchanted team members listen to each other in a way that restores—and builds—trust. Often, team members start thinking of their team as people they care about and who care about them. (Many times they tell us that the practices improve their family life, too.) They have honest conversations and give ongoing feedback that makes each other better. They trust each other more. They collaborate well. They relate to teammates as coaches, and there's more of a sense of "we" than "I." They look out for each other. They don't have as many meetings, but when they do, things get done. They act with integrity.

At first, incorporating these practices may feel awkward or seem hard. You might think the discipline takes too much time or distracts you from "real work." But by committing to these practices, you will be energized by how quickly your workday becomes easier. People get (a lot) more done, in less time. Work stops landing back on your desk. Upon completing projects, you'll notice a team pride that wasn't there before.

But the levels of achievement and enjoyment that come from applying these practices can only be known *once you've tried them*. With intention and effort comes the reward—a high-performance team.

Keep in mind that the shift to high-performance is an ongoing choice. Your team will slip, even after incorporating what you've learned here. It's only human to fall out of practice sometimes. You might notice the team isn't collaborating as well, or the momentum has become lackluster. When you begin to see warning signs like this, immediately return to the practice you feel will best recalibrate the team.

Be patient with yourself and with each other. Try things out, experiment, and adapt the practices to best suit your team. Think of ways to teach the skillsets in this book to others in your organization. The more people in your company share the language of high performance, the greater the capability for cross-departmental collaboration. Teams with conflicting agendas will quickly unite over a common purpose. The more your entire organization applies the practices, the more phenomenal the results, as measured by revenues, productivity, and overall well-being of employees. We know this to be true because we see it time and again in the companies we work with.

Succeeding as a business takes vision, grit, determination, and an incredible ability to work together. With the practices in this book, you'll know how to come together as a team to accomplish anything. You'll have more bandwidth to work on the *real* work, not the interpersonal difficulties that make things tough and slow you down. You'll love your work, and your team will, too. You'll achieve wild success. We've had clients tell us, "We couldn't have done what we did without this stuff," and, "A lot of the problems we had before just aren't there anymore," and even, "Doing this changed my life."

We believe *you* will find yourself feeling this way, too, because adopting these practices is a powerful way to invest in yourself and your company.

Companies have a financial journey, and they have a leadership journey. A CEO knows their financial journey starts with creating a strategy and executing the plan by implementing systems to scale financially over time. However, it's equally important to prioritize your leadership journey. A leadership journey is like the DNA of a company—it's a cultural effort that requires a shared language of how to communicate and lead effectively across teams and departments.

Without a scalable leadership DNA, you're likely leaving results on the table. You might make money, but you'll see a lot of wasted resources, cross-functional projects moving at a snail's pace, and a work culture that sags around the middle. It would be the equivalent of not upgrading your computers and software for ten years and wondering why you can't compete. The reason CEOS and PE companies insist on bringing us in is they know the financial journey is table stakes; the real differentiator is consistently scaling a shared language of leadership practices in their company to optimize their teams. For the companies we work with, CEOS and investors know that scaling leadership is not a class, a book, or a learning management system; it is the practices used every day in the hallways and Zoom calls of great organizations. Apply the practices in this book, and you will join that exceptional group.

Finally, don't take our word for any of this. Try it out. Ask yourself, "Which practice would be helpful in my situation?" Come back to the book as your reference. Modify what you read and find a way to apply it to your specific circumstance. The practices are intended to be used as you see fit and can be applied to almost any situation.

Good luck on your road to high performance. Let us know how it goes.

RESOURCES

1   Harbir Singh, "Why Do So Many Mergers Fail?" *Knowledge at Wharton*, The Wharton School at the University of Pennsylvania, March 30, 2005, https://knowledge.wharton.upenn.edu/article/why-do-so-many-mergers-fail/.

2   Global Human Capital Trends, "The New Organization: Different by Design," Deloitte Insights, 2016, https://www2.deloitte.com/us/en/insights/multimedia/infographics/2016-human-capital-trends.html.

3   Kotter, "Does Corporate Culture Drive Financial Performance?" *Forbes*, February 10, 2011, https://www.forbes.com/sites/johnkotter/2011/02/10/does-corporate-culture-drive-financial-performance/?sh=7a478a487e9e.

4   Peter F. Drucker, *The Practice of Management* (New York: Harper and Row, 1954).

5   Michael Jordan, during a TV interview with former Georgetown basketball coach John Thompson, which aired on TNT in February 2003.

6   Seth Stevenson, "A Rare Joint Interview with Microsoft CEO Satya Nadella and Bill Gates," *Wall Street Journal*, September 25, 2017, https://www.wsj.com/articles/a-rare-joint-interview-with-microsoft-ceo-satya-nadella-and-bill-gates-1506358852.

7   Will Felps, Terence Mitchell, and Eliza Byington, "How, When, and Why Bad Apples Spoil the Barrel: Negative Group Members and

Dysfunctional Groups," *Research in Organizational Behavior* 27 (2006): 175–222, https://doi.org/10.1016/S0191-3085(06)27005-9.

8 John Tierney and Roy F. Baumeister, *The Power of Bad: How the Negativity Effect Rules Us and How We Can Rule It* (New York: Penguin Books, 2019).

9 Julie Tseng and Jordan Poppenk, "Brain Meta-State Transitions Demarcate Thoughts across Task Contexts Exposing the Mental Noise of Trait Neuroticism," *Nature Communications* 11, no. 3480 (July 2020), v.

10 H. A. Dorfman, *The Mental Game of Baseball: A Guide to Peak Performance* (Lanham, MD: Diamond Communications, 2002).

11 Viktor E. Frankl, *Man's Search for Meaning* (Boston: Beacon Press, 2006).

12 Stephen B. Karpman, *A Game Free Life: The New Transactional Analysis of Intimacy, Openness, and Happiness* (San Francisco: Drama Triangle Publications, 2014).

13 David Emerald, *The Power of TED* (*The Empowerment Dynamic)* (Chicago: Polaris Publishing, 2005).

14 Maya Angelou, *Wouldn't Take Nothing for My Journey Now* (New York: Bantam, 1994).

15 Robert Greenleaf, *Servant Leadership: A Journey into the Nature of Legitimate Power and Greatness* (Mahwah, NJ: Paulist Press, 1977).

16 "Guide: Understand Team Effectiveness," re:Work, accessed August 30, 2022, https://rework.withgoogle.com/print/guides/5721312655835136/.

17 Igor Pistelak, "Performance vs. Trust by Simon Sinek," Profit Circles, December 3, 2019, https://www.profit-circles.com/new-blog/2019/12/3/performance-vs-trust-by-simon-sinek.

18 People Driven Performance, "Cost of Poor Internal Communications: Business Case for Effective Internal Communications, 2014" (PowerPoint presentation, September 20, 2012), https://www.slideshare.net/ldickmeyer/cost-of-poor-internal-communications-912.

19 The Economist Intelligence Unit and Lucidchart, *Communication Barriers in the Modern Workplace* (2018), https://eiuperspectives.economist.com/sites/default/files/EIU_Lucidchart-Communication%20barriers%20in%20the%20modern%20workplace.pdf.

20 William V. Haney, *Communication and Interpersonal Relations: Text and Cases* (Homewood, IL: Irwin, 1979).

21 Lisa O'Malley, "8 Corporate Culture Statistics That'll Change How

You Treat Employees," Bonfyre, accessed August 30, 2022, https://bonfyreapp.com/blog/8-stats-building-a-corporate-culture.

22 Daniel Coyle, *The Culture Code: The Secrets of Highly Successful Groups* (New York: Bantam, 2018).

23 Patrick Lencioni, *The Five Dysfunctions of a Team: A Leadership Fable* (San Francisco: Jossey-Bass, 2002).

24 Steve Crabtree, "Worldwide, 13% of Employees Are Engaged at Work," Gallup, October 8, 2013, https://news.gallup.com/poll/165269/worldwide-employees-engaged-work.aspx.

25 Peter Senge, *The Fifth Discipline: The Art & Practice of the Learning Organization* (New York: Doubleday, 1990).

26 Lencioni, *Five Dysfunctions of a Team.*

27 Simon Sinek, *Start with Why: How Great Leaders Inspire Everyone to Take Action* (New York: Portfolio, 2009).

28 John Mackey, "Former Housemates John Mackey and Kip Tindell Talk about Poker, Retailing, and the Limitations of Shareholder Capitalism," interview by Kip Tindell, *TIME*, June 26, 2008, https://business.time.com/2008/06/26/former_housemates_john_mackey/.

29 Senge, *Fifth Discipline.*

30 Daniel H. Pink, *Drive: The Surprising Truth About What Motivates Us* (New York: Riverhead Books, 2011).

31 Marcus Buckingham and Ashley Goodall, "The Feedback Fallacy," *Harvard Business Review*, March–April, 2019, https://hbr.org/2019/03/the-feedback-fallacy.

32 Buckingham and Goodall, "The Feedback Fallacy."

33 Dictionary.com, s.v. "feedback (n.)," accessed August 31, 2022, https://www.dictionary.com/browse/feedback.

34 Ken Blanchard, "Feedback Is the Breakfast of Champions," Ken Blanchard Books, August 17, 2009, https://www.kenblanchardbooks.com/feedback-is-the-breakfast-of-champions/.

35 Ben Wigert and Nate Dvorak, "Feedback Is Not Enough," Gallup, May 16, 2019, https://www.gallup.com/workplace/257582/feedback-not-enough.aspx.

36 Robert Sutton and Ben Wigert, "More Harm Than Good: The Truth

About Performance Reviews," Gallup, May 6, 2019, https://www.gallup.com/workplace/249332/harm-good-truth-performance-reviews.aspx.

37 Sutton and Wigert, "More Harm Than Good."

38 Stevenson, "A Rare Joint Interview."

39 Jim Harter and Amy Adkins, "Employees Want a Lot More From Their Managers," Gallup, April 8, 2015, https://www.gallup.com/workplace/236570/employees-lot-managers.aspx.

40 W. Timothy Gallwey, *The Inner Game of Tennis: The Classic Guide to the Mental Side of Peak Performance* (New York: Random House Trade Paperbacks, 1997).

41 Mihaly Csikszentmihalyi, *Flow: The Psychology of Optimal Performance* (New York: Harper Perennial, 1990).

42 Kim Scott, *Radical Candor: Be a Kick-Ass Boss Without Losing Your Humanity* (New York: St. Martin's Press, 2017).

43 John Mackey, "How to Succeed by Being Authentic (Hint: Carefully)," November 4, 2020, in interview *Freakonomics Radio*, produced by Rebecca Lee Douglas, podcast, audio, 47:31, https://freakonomics.com/podcast/john-mackey/.

44 Coyle, *Culture Code*.

45 Lillian Cunningham, "Trying to Change the World Bank," *The Washington Post*, April 10, 2014, https://www.washingtonpost.com/news/on-leadership/wp/2014/04/10/trying-to-change-the-world-bank/.

46 Reed Hastings and Erin Meyer, *No Rules Rules: Netflix and the Culture of Reinvention* (New York: Penguin Press, 2020).

47 Scott, *Radical Candor*.

48 Holmes Report, "The Cost of Poor Communications," PRovoke Media, July 16, 2011, https://www.provokemedia.com/latest/article/the-cost-of-poor-communications.

49 Victor Lipman, "All Successful Leaders Need This Quality: Self-Awareness," *Forbes*, November 18, 2013, https://www.forbes.com/sites/victorlipman/2013/11/18/all-successful-leaders-need-this-quality-self-awareness/?sh=7287477b1f06.

50 Frankki Bevins and Aaron De Smet, "Making Time Management the Organization's Priority," *McKinsey Quarterly*, January 1, 2013, https://www.mckinsey.com/capabilities/people-and-organizational-performance/our-

insights/making-time-management-the-organizations-priority

51 Richard Koch, *The 80/20 Manager: The Secret to Working Less and Achieving More* (Boston: Little, Brown and Company, 2013).

52 Stephen R. Covey, *The 7 Habits of Highly Effective People: Powerful Lessons in Personal Change* (New York: Free Press, 1989).

53 J. D. Meier, *Getting Results the Agile Way: A Personal Results System for Work and Life* (Bellevue, WA: Innovation Playhouse, 2010).

54 Koch, *80/20 Principle*.

55 Patrick Lencioni, *The Motive: Why So Many Leaders Abdicate Their Most Important Responsibilities* (Hoboken: Wiley, 2020).

56 Matt Martin, "The State of Meetings in 2020," Clockwise, February 10, 2020, https://www.getclockwise.com/blog/the-state-of-meetings-in-2020.

57 Ari Weinzweig, *Zingerman's Guide to Good Leading, Part 1: A Lapsed Anarchist's Approach to Building a Great Business* (Ann Arbor: Zingerman's Press, 2010).

58 Cameron Herold, *Double Double: How to Double Your Revenue and Profit in 3 Years or Less* (Austin: Greenleaf Book Group Press, 2011).

59 Kenneth Chenault is famously credited for saying this quote; however, the original citation could not be found.

60 Chris McGoff, *The Primes: How Any Group Can Solve Any Problem* (Hoboken: Wiley, 2012).

61 PRNewswire, "Do American Workers Need a Vacation? New CareerBuilder Data Shows Majority Are Burned Out at Work, While Some Are Highly Stressed or Both," press release, CareerBuilder, May 23, 2017, https://press.careerbuilder.com/2017-05-23-Do-American-Workers-Need-a-Vacation-New-CareerBuilder-Data-Shows-Majority-Are-Burned-Out-at-Work-While-Some-Are-Highly-Stressed-or-Both.

62 Britta K. Hölzel et al., "Mindfulness Practice Leads to Increases in Regional Brain Gray Matter Density," *Psychology Research* 191, no. 1 (January 2011): 36–43, https://doi.org/10.1016/j.pscychresns.2010.08.006.

63 Bevins and De Smet, "Making Time Management the Organization's Priority."

64 Csikszentmihalyi, *Flow*.

65 McGoff, *The Primes*.

66 Tierney and Baumeister, *The Power of Bad*.

67 Lencioni, *Five Dysfunctions of a Team*.

ACKNOWLEDGMENTS

We wrote this book because we're inspired by people who want to make a difference in the world—those with vision who overcome insurmountable challenges to accomplish great things. Thank you to everyone who prioritizes the well-being of others in service of your goals, who builds businesses and finds solutions that make our world a better place. For those who lead with heart, listen with care, and build work cultures where others thrive: thank you.

It is with great humility that we add our own perspective to the canon of books on leadership. We could not have learned what we have without the incredible ingenuity, grit, and wisdom of our clients. Thank you to each of you who have trusted us with your confidence and friendship.

To our team of dedicated BLUECASE coaches and consultants: thank you for your commitment to transforming the lives of everyone you coach. It takes a profound dedication to show up day after day to help leaders work through their struggles. We honor you. It makes it easy for us to stay on track when we get to work with people we love so much.

To Christine Trevino, our third musketeer, you are the rock of our company. We could not be where we are if you hadn't shown up at the time you did and walked with us over the years. Thank you for your ongoing leadership, friendship, and support. You are a remarkable superwoman.

Thank you to everyone who has helped turn this book into what it is. Special thanks to Justin's mom, Mary, who, besides being endlessly caring and tireless in her support, is also an exceptional editor. Without you, this book would have fallen flat. Thank you for all you do (and for teaching Justin how to read and write!) We hope this book makes you proud.

To Christel Frietsch, for your positivity and dedication to our company, and, in particular, for managing the details of getting this massive book project over the finish line. Thank you!

Thank you to our professional editor, Maria Gagliano, who took this book from good to great. We were extremely lucky to benefit from your intuitive expertise and fine-tuned focus. To Caitlin McIntosh, thank you for providing your design expertise, your years of friendship, and your commitment to depth and wisdom. Thank you, also, Chris Rorrer for the original cover design and to Sarah Brody for bringing it to life. And thank you to our team at Scribe, especially Meghan McCracken, who has supported our project for years with a steady enthusiasm, guidance, and intelligence that made all the difference, and Juliane Bergmann, who jumped in to support the finishing touches with excellence and exuberance.

Thank you to all our mentors who have helped shape our own ability to lead. Thank you, especially, to Peter, who taught us to have grace and humility in the face of the storms life brings; to Khotso, who led in service of a more loving world; to J.R., without whom BLUECASE might not exist; and to Marie and Gary, who in many ways have been the godparents of our company. We are beyond grateful to have been blessed with such a supportive community of advocates.

To Justin's brother, Sean, thank you for epitomizing what it means to be family and for a bond far beyond brotherhood. To David's wife, Julia, and daughters, Evie and Eliana, thank you for bringing the joy of family and fatherhood to David's life. To David's mom Jayne, brother Adam, sister Alexandra, Chantel, Bailey, Will, Trey, Jim, Nathanael, Adam, Ian, Chris, Josh, Nic, Jonathan, Rhoda, Carolyn, Brooke, and Jordan, thank you. Your support, counsel, and friendship in our lives have made us better people.

Finally, we would like to thank Justin's father, Greg, and David's late father, Eric. While we may falter at times, we both aspire to be good men leading lives of integrity and service. For both of us, the seed of this aspiration was planted by our dads, whose love, care, guidance, and support inspire us to do the best we can in all we do.

For more information on how BLUECASE can create culture change and develop high-performing teams at *your* organization, please reach out at *info@bluecase.com*.

SUPER BOOST YOUR PRACTICES: EXERCISE AND MEDITATION

Your team's well-being directly reflects its individual team members' well-being. Unfortunately, most teams in fast-growth companies are plagued by the same issue: burnout stress levels. According to Career Builder's research of over three thousand US employees, 61 percent of workers say they're burned out in their current job, and 31 percent report high levels of work stress.[61]

Stress impedes focus, overwhelms the nervous system, and leads to burnout. Too much stress in the body is correlated with both physical and mental health issues. No matter how strong your work team is, you are only as capable as your body and mind will allow.

Fortunately, there is a way to improve your energy, decrease your stress, and get "into the zone": mindfulness meditation combined with exercise. Most people know that relaxation and exercise make you feel better when you're stressed out and have low energy. One director we worked with complained repeatedly about job stress. Even his face looked tired. At the beginning of our coaching sessions, he agreed (reluctantly) to meditate five minutes each day and add three days of weight training per week. By the end of six weeks, he was practically glowing. He'd lost ten pounds and was standing more upright. He also noticed he was doing less and accomplishing more at work. (And a month later, he met his new girlfriend!)

It rarely fails: anyone who follows a simple routine experiences significant results in six weeks. It doesn't take a lot of effort, but if you haven't been meditating and exercising already, getting started may be a challenge for you. Muscle through the first week or so, and it will get easier. You might even like it. You'll also start noticing improvements at work. In our coaching practice, we find that those who commit to a simple regimen of meditation and exercise advance more quickly than those who don't.

FIGHT, FLIGHT, OR FREEZE

Your body's nervous system is designed to protect you. When you're in a dangerous situation, it activates the sympathetic nervous system, commonly referred to as "fight, flight, or freeze" (we talked about this briefly in Chapter 4). Should a wild, predatory animal creep up behind you, you'll feel an immediate jolt, compliments of your sympathetic nervous system. You immediately prepare to defend yourself, run away, or go into a frozen state like deer in headlights. Your adrenal glands pump cortisol and adrenaline into your body, and with repeated exposure to this reaction over time, you experience exhaustion and overwhelm (i.e., burnout).

In your work environment, there (probably) aren't any tigers threatening your survival. But every confrontation with a coworker, concern about a deadline, frustrating criticism, or disappointment puts your sympathetic nervous system on high alert. Anytime we feel that charge of anger, worry, or overwhelm at work, fight, flight, or freeze kicks in. Our bodies become used to this state, and after a while, we can't get out of it. The underlying anxiety and agitation we've become accustomed to is the result of the "protective" mechanisms of a sympathetic nervous system that's always activated.

When you go on a long, relaxing vacation, you feel like sixty pounds have been lifted from your shoulders. You breathe easier. The stress is gone. If only you could feel like this all the time! But you know when you go back to work, that heaviness will pack right back on—possibly the moment you sit down to your computer.

The ease you feel on your vacation is your body shifting from an activated sympathetic nervous system to your parasympathetic nervous system. The parasympathetic nervous system is often described as "rest and digest." This is your body's programmed way of saying you're out of harm's way. You no longer need to divert your energy into protecting yourself. Your heart rate goes down, breathing slows, and you can rest and digest your food.

The parasympathetic nervous system also correlates with higher levels of ingenuity and creative problem-solving. When you're not in fight, flight, or freeze mode, you have more energy to spend on big-picture innovations and solutions instead of "firefighting" emergencies. You more easily enter a state of flow at work.

Even when you aren't on vacation, you can drastically reduce your stress levels and increase your focus with exercise and meditation. These disciplines really do make everything better. For this reason, we encourage teams to make health and well-being a shared accountability. The better you feel, the less likely you'll get stuck in fight, flight, or freeze. The benefits of a meditation practice, specifically, combat stress while increasing focus and performance—a big reason the 2014 Super Bowl–winning Seattle Seahawks coach Pete Carroll hired a meditation coach to work with his team.

Encourage each other to put a few hours of de-stressing activities on the calendar and stick to them.

EXERCISE

When it comes to exercise, twenty minutes, three times a week of vigorous physical activity has been proven to reduce stress and anxiety, boost moods, and improve overall performance. Usually, when we work with a CEO who is overly stressed, the first thing we do is suggest she focus on an exercise program. If you've been saying to yourself, "I know I should exercise more," then you probably need to.

There's not much more to say about this one but, "Get it on your calendar."

MEDITATE

Over the past fifteen years, evidence for the stress-reducing effectiveness of a meditation practice continues to grow, which is why companies like Google have implemented meditation training in their leadership development program.

As stress goes down, focus, creativity, and performance improve.

For most of our clients, we recommend a secular form of meditation called Mindfulness-Based Stress Reduction (MBSR), or mindful body scans. This is the practice of bringing your attention to different body parts and allowing each to relax. You literally teach your body to de-stress, part by part. At the Center for Stress Reduction at the University of Massachusetts, researchers found that when subjects practiced mindful body relaxation each day for eight weeks, stress and anxiety dropped substantially.[62] Additionally, their body's natural healing capacity increased.

Our experience corroborates this. When individuals we work with commit to a daily mindfulness practice of as little as two to three minutes a day, they experience a change in how they feel in a few short weeks.

Sometimes, a meditation practice intimidates people or bores them. They say, "My mind is too busy for this." But the goal of this kind of meditation is not to stop your mind. Rather, it's to teach your body to relax (and over time, your mind will, too). Regular practice allows you to spend more time in the parasympathetic state versus fight, flight, or freeze. Imagine being able to invoke that "vacation feeling" whenever you want to!

Meditation doesn't take a lot of time. If you commit to a mindfulness practice for as little as two minutes each day, you'll notice a change. While there are countless free resources to help you learn a mindfulness practice, the five simple steps below are all you need. *You will notice a difference if you practice as little as two minutes of meditation each day.* You can do it in your office. You can do it anytime you feel stress increase. You can even do it right now:

1. In your chair, close your eyes and take three full deep breaths all the way into your stomach.
2. Relax your jaw and shoulders.

3. Bring your attention to your feet on the ground.

4. Feel the feelings of your seat in the chair.

5. Notice your breath in your belly and slow down your breathing for two to three minutes.

Notice a difference?

If you're interested in an easy way to try out different kinds of guided meditation, we recommend exploring the variety of free apps available to download onto any device.

A SHARED LANGUAGE OF HIGH PERFORMANCE

80/20 actions: Actions or priorities that, if you focus on them, will bring about the greatest gains.

10,000-foot conversation: A conversation that assesses the big picture of your current state with input from all team members.

actions conversation: A conversation where you decide who is doing what by when.

Big 3 Goals: The three actions that will yield 80 percent of your results.

blaming mindset: A mindset wherein you continually find fault in others.

Both/And: A high-performance approach to conversations that involves deep listening so that all perspectives are considered. The open dialogue that results is a characteristic of high-performance teams.[63]

challenger mindset: A mindset that challenges another person's mediocrity and calls forth their greatness.

checking in: Giving each person a few minutes to speak at the beginning of a meeting to share how they're doing.

clarity-oriented person: Cites facts when they bring forward an idea. They are thorough in their reporting and presentations. They present all the facts and push back when not enough details have been considered.

coach mindset: A mindset that has you thinking about ways to support others to fix their own problems.

coaching style of leadership: Feedback that leads to performance improvement.

collective point of view (executive point of view): Seeing the organization as a whole, not only from the perspective of one person's own function. It allows teams to operate as "greater than the sum of their parts."

complaining mindset: A mindset that makes one feel they are a victim of their situation.

connection-oriented person: Talks a lot about people, big ideas, and feelings. They socialize ideas across the organization and make sure everyone is in the loop in their communications.

constructive negative feedback: Honest feedback on what a person needs to work on to improve their performance.

creator mindset: A mindset that asks, "What is the specific outcome I/we want? What baby step could we try to get us there?"

decision registry: A record of all decisions made in a meeting.

deep listening: A high-skill form of listening that quickly builds trust, deepens connection, and ensures communication has taken place.

delay: Actions that can be put on hold.

delegate: Actions that can be passed on to someone else on the team.

delete: Actions that, when looked at objectively, no longer need to be done.

disempowered mindset: A mindset that leads to disempowered actions.

Either/Or: An approach to conversations that leads to binary decision-making. This can keep people locked into right and wrong, which blocks the ability to find common ground and have an open dialogue.

empowered mindset: A mindset that leads a person to take powerful actions.

feedback listening tours: One-on-one interviews conducted to gather feedback, insight, and information. The person asking for feedback is there to *listen*, not to debate or solve problems on the spot.

flow state: Peak performance state, where every action, movement, and thought follows inevitably from the previous one.[64]

Fundamental Why: The underlying purpose or intention.

future-telling: A brainstorming exercise where the team imagines their desired vision has already happened.

impact-oriented person: Talks a lot about the big picture. They want to set big goals, move quickly, and talk about results.

integrity: Say → Do[65]

intrinsic motivation: An internal driver, rather than an external incentive like money or fame.

listening to understand: A form of deep listening that builds stronger relationships based on empathy.

mindset: Your way of thinking, which leads to your way of acting.

negativity bias: The universal tendency for negative events and emotions to affect us more strongly than positive ones.[66]

options conversation: A conversation that explores all the different possible approaches to addressing what's in your way to move toward your vision.

parking lot: A record of off-topic issues that arise in a meeting.

Personal Fundamental Why: An individual's underlying purpose for why they do what they do.

planning to get things done: A five-step routine that ensures new initiatives are completed.

playing what ifs: A brainstorming exercise where everyone on the team offers suggestions for how to address what's currently in the way.

psychological safety: When teams trust and respect each other and speak freely about concerns, ideas, and mistakes without the fear of negative consequences.

rabbit holes: Subjects that are off-topic from a meeting's Fundamental Why.

rescuer mindset: A mindset that has one trying to fix everyone else's problems.

self-awareness: A willingness and ability to take an honest look at yourself.

solutions-oriented feedback: Feedback that offers clear, ongoing suggestions for improvement.

strengths-based feedback: Feedback that focuses on what someone already does well.

structure-oriented person: The process planners and architects who focus on how to accomplish something. They are practical in how they talk and don't want to spend much time talking about how people feel.

team agility: A team's ability to draw on their strengths and compensate for their weaknesses.

vision of wild success: A vision that describes an *unpredictable future.*

visual display: Written plans for getting things done.

vulnerability-based trust: A form of trust that builds when team members make themselves vulnerable to one another and can be confident that their respective vulnerabilities will not be used against them.[67]

LEADERSHIP AND CULTURAL COMPANY ASSESSMENT

Assess how well your company is doing with this short assessment (adapted from the complete survey we use to assess company performance). We typically ask everyone in the company to complete this and include one-on-one interviews, but to get a quick read on your company's leadership, answer the questions below.

For more insight on how your organization scores in terms of leadership and company culture, you can find our full Company Assessment tool at *betterteambook.com*.

Add up your score. Consider that a consolidated score of 85 percent or higher is a strong score. Anything below 85 percent is considered average to poor, and likely indicates mediocre performance.

LEADERSHIP CULTURE ASSESSMENT

Score your company 1–10 (1 = strongly disagree, 10 = strongly agree)

1. Our managers, directors, and executives know how to get the best out of their direct reports.

    O O O O O O O O O O
    1 2 3 4 5 6 7 8 9 10

2. Our managers are capable leaders who will be able to steer the company in the future.

    O O O O O O O O O O
    1 2 3 4 5 6 7 8 9 10

3. Employees consistently take ownership of initiatives and drive them to completion.

    O O O O O O O O O O
    1 2 3 4 5 6 7 8 9 10

4. The company actively and effectively develops the leadership capability of all employees.

    O O O O O O O O O O
    1 2 3 4 5 6 7 8 9 10

5. The meetings I attend are necessary, highly effective, and collaborative. They have a clear purpose and agenda.

    O O O O O O O O O O
    1 2 3 4 5 6 7 8 9 10

6. Our team feels safe to regularly take risks without feeling insecure, afraid to fail, or embarrassed.

    O O O O O O O O O O
    1 2 3 4 5 6 7 8 9 10

7. Employees receive feedback on a weekly basis that helps them perform better.

    O O O O O O O O O O
    1 2 3 4 5 6 7 8 9 10

8. On work-related topics, team members feel confident expressing views contrary to the dominant viewpoint of senior leaders.

    O O O O O O O O O O
    1 2 3 4 5 6 7 8 9 10

9. Conflicts in our organization are skillfully resolved.

    O O O O O O O O O O
    1 2 3 4 5 6 7 8 9 10

10. Cross-functional projects happen effortlessly and seamlessly.

    O O O O O O O O O O
    1 2 3 4 5 6 7 8 9 10

ABOUT BLUECASE

Justin Follin and David Butlein Greenspan, PhD, are co-founders of BLUECASE, a leadership and strategic planning consultancy headquartered in Austin, Texas.

Jet fuel comes in blue cases, and the work BLUECASE does is like jet fuel for companies that want to achieve more. We work with CEOS and their companies, venture capitalists, and private equity firms who have a "fire in their belly" but are frustrated they can't accomplish what they *know* is possible. Our clients are mission-driven, hungry for greatness, and truly care about their customers and employees.

Drawing from David's PhD in Psychology and our collective background in high-performance management consulting, we embed the habits, mindsets, and tools of high-performance individuals and teams into everything we do. As a result, we have amassed a significant set of outcomes and experiences in wildly successful, fast-growth companies, some of which look like this:

- A technology company worth $10M when we started working with them in 2013 sold for over 70 times that when they exited. It was one of the largest exits in Austin, Texas, for the year they sold. Today they are a global company, vastly outperforming their competitors, known as a great place to work, and valued at over a billion dollars.

- A client in the lifestyle space quadrupled their top and bottom line in seven years, becoming one of the largest US companies in their sector, while their CEO won the Ernst and Young Entrepreneur of the Year award.

- A consulting business we worked with for seven years sold for 2.4 times the revenue with no earn-out even though they had $0 in recurring revenue (most companies in their space sell for a multiple of EBITDA).

- A Peter Thiel–backed robotics startup raising capital for its series B funding round when COVID-19 hit, lost their investment partner. Shortly thereafter, working with us to reorganize, they were funded by one of the largest cleaning product companies in the world.

- A 150-person financial company we worked with was purchased during the pandemic by one of the top Fintech companies in the US. The acquired company and its CEO are now seen as the central growth engine of the 35,000-plus-person acquiring company.

While we're industry agnostic, we tend to work with visionary disruptors, innovators, change makers, and creative entrepreneurs who see "what could be" and whose companies are making a positive impact on the world. The companies we work with are fast-scaling and innovative. When the tools and skills we teach are integrated into companies like these, a "jet-fuel effect" happens. They innovate, grow, and respond faster and more intelligently than their competitors, attract top talent, and are known in their industries as great places to work.

You can learn how fast-growth companies apply these proven concepts and methods from high-performance psychology so you can apply them in your business. Start by taking the 5-minute Company Assessment at *bluecase.com/betterteam*.

ABOUT THE AUTHORS

Justin Follin is a lifelong student and teacher of what brings out the best in people and a trusted advisor to leaders in fast-growth business sectors. Along with co-author and founder **David Butlein Greenspan**, Justin is the co-founder and managing partner of BLUECASE Strategic Partners. Drawing from David's PhD in high-performance psychology and their combined twenty-five years of organizational consulting expertise, Justin and David specialize in solving leadership cultural problems that inevitably come with scale. They have successfully coached CEOs and leadership teams in publicly traded companies and in rapidly scaling, private-equity backed businesses ranging from $20M to $2B in revenue.

Printed in the USA
CPSIA information can be obtained
at www.ICGtesting.com
LVHW040300121023
760735LV00002B/3/J